VIETNAM

THE UNFORGETTABLE TRAGEDY

BOOKS BY JOSEPH BUTTINGER

IN THE TWILIGHT OF SOCIALISM:
A History of the Revolutionary Socialists of Austria (1953)

THE SMALLER DRAGON:
A Political History of Vietnam (1958)

VIETNAM: A DRAGON EMBATTLED (1967)

VIETNAM: A POLITICAL HISTORY (1968)

A DRAGON DEFIANT:
A Short History of Vietnam (1972)

VIETNAM

THE UNFORGETTABLE TRAGEDY

Joseph Buttinger

HORIZON PRESS
NEW YORK

Library of Congress Catalog No.: 76-20309
ISBN: 0-8180-0820-2
Manufactured in the United States of America

To the many young American victims
of this tragedy—those who fought
and those who refused to fight in Vietnam

Contents

Illustrations

Preface

Vietnam: The Unforgettable Tragedy, unlike my previous five volumes on Vietnam, was not written primarily to supply a record of historical events up to the end of the struggle for Indochina in April 1975. These highly dramatic events will be recorded here as accurately as I could ascertain them. But what was secondary in my earlier work—interpretations of events in order to bring about a more sophisticated American policy toward Indochina—is my primary objective in this book. This is one of the reasons why, more than anything else I have written on Vietnam, it is highly polemical. Notwithstanding my efforts to make it accurate as history, *Vietnam: The Unforgettable Tragedy* is essentially a political treatise.

In telling what actually happened in Indochina since the end of World War II, my emphasis remains, from beginning to end, why it happened and why the two Indochina wars—French and American—ended as they did.

Why did the United States, disregarding its claim to be anticolonial, support the war of colonial reconquest which France started in Vietnam in September 1945? Why, after the failure of France to defeat the Communist-led Vietnamese movement of national liberation, did the United States, under five presidents for over twenty-one years, waste billions and kill millions in an attempt to succeed where France had failed? And now that all is over, more important than any other question: What can the American people, and especially a new generation of political leaders, learn from our country's ill-advised involvement in the struggle for Indochina, and from the failure of its costly and brutal effort to maintain a viable anti-Communist state in South Vietnam?

A country's foreign policy may be correctly motivated, decently pursued and yet remain unsuccessful. But America's Vietnam policy would have been no less wrong if Washington had succeeded in achieving its ill-chosen aims. Once to-day's passions have subsided, the vast majority of the American people, I am sure, will condemn this policy, not only for obvious humanitarian reasons, but also from short-term political and long-term historical points of view.

The fact that many Americans who supported this policy were decently motivated makes it only more urgent to search for an answer to the question how this inhumane, politically erroneous and in the last analysis stupid course could be pursued for many years by a country so rich in knowledgeable people, high intelligence and good will. These, unfortunately, do not always occupy the centers of power where decisions of consequence for the nation, and for the world, are being made. Vietnam has provided abundant evidence that the decisions of too many of our political leaders were based on ignorance; that others believed all means, no matter how brutal, are justified in the pursuit of American political goals; that lack of political courage prevented not a few from revising mistaken decisions even after they had recognized them as such; and, worst of all, that there are also those who did not hesitate consciously to deceive the American people about Vietnam in order not to lose political support.

To answer the questions raised by America's failure in Vietnam and to fairly apportion responsibility for it, makes it necessary to reveal the ignorance of some important Americans, to condemn the brutality of others, to deplore the cowardice and denounce the deceptions of everyone guilty of these political sins.

However, this depressing but necessary record of defective American political leadership I shall balance by quoting from other people—including some courageous politicians—who effectively criticized our Vietnam policy, some from the very beginning of our intervention, others after the United States went to war in Vietnam, and others only when they recognized that the war could not be won.

In quoting so many authors critical of what America has done in Indochina, especially since February 1965, I not only try to assemble what I consider sophisticated support for my own views. Other reasons are to acknowledge what I owe to these authors in writing this book, and to tell readers less familiar with over two decades of discussion about Vietnam how many intelligent, patriotic and courageous Americans, often at the risk of being denounced as pro-Communist and anti-American, opposed a policy which today even its most prominent advocates rarely venture to defend.

I include a brief chapter about myself in order to correct a few mistaken views and distorted facts about my own involvement with Vietnam—not as a student of history but as a so-called "lobbyist" and "adviser" of the South Vietnamese President Ngo Dinh Diem.

The number of people I have to quote in this book is exceptionally large. Unless otherwise stated, *The New Republic* of May 3, 1975 is the source of all quotations from:

Dong Duc Khoi
Stanley Hoffman
James Chace
Richard Holbrooke
Ronald Steel
Hans Morgenthau
Harold Isaacs
Frances FitzGerald
Chester L. Cooper
Anthony Lewis
Stanley Karnow
George McT. Kahin

Again, unless otherwise stated, *The New York Review of Books* of June 12, 1975 is the source of all quotations from

> Geoffrey Barraclough
> Robert Lowell
> Noam Chomsky
> Mary McCarthy
> Norman Mailer
> J. M. Cameron
> Christopher Lasch
> John F. Fairbank
> Stuart Hampshire
> George Kennan
> Susan Sontag

The same applies to the many quotations from Robert Shaplen, which with a few exceptions are all taken from *The New Yorker* of May 19, 1975.

The number of persons (mostly American) whose statements I quoted in support of or in opposition to the Vietnamese war is 170, which adds up to a useful record of what prominent and influential Americans thought about their country's involvement in the struggle for Indochina.

PART *One*

From 1945 To 1965

I.
Vietnam In 1945

It has long been my contention that ignorance of Vietnamese history was one of the reasons the United States pursued a policy which, in its complete disregard of the political realities of contemporary Vietnam, was doomed to fail. It was bad enough not to take into consideration that the Vietnamese people had struggled for over two thousand years against being absorbed by China, and had for almost one hundred years fought against colonial rule in order to regain independence. Much worse still was not to know, or knowingly to disregard, the fact that as a result of French colonial policies in Indochina the whole of Vietnam had become Communist by the end of World War II.

I say the whole of Vietnam, not only the North—something which, in spite of thirty years of French and American propaganda, remains an undeniable historical fact. Moreover, Communist control of the whole country was achieved without the use of force, not of course because the Vietnamese Communists reject force as a means to gain power, but for the simple reason that in the absence of any effective political resistance, the Communists needed no force to establish control over the whole of Vietnam. The need to use force arose only later. Anti-Communist nationalists returned from exile together with the hated Chinese Nationalist army of occupation only after Communist control had been established, and then achieved, under Chinese military protection, control of a few northern prov-inces. When the Chinese army, in June of 1946, was withdrawn from northern Vietnam, the Communist Vietminh leaders at Hanoi had not the slightest hesitation in eliminating these nationalist en-claves by force.

Nothing proves more convincingly the ease with which the Communists achieved control over the whole country than the deci-sions taken by leading non-Communists in Hué and Saigon only days after the Vietminh had made themselves masters at Hanoi. In March 1945, when the Japanese in Indochina abolished the French administration (which had submissively collaborated with them), Vietnam became nominally independent, under a Japanese-tolerated national government at the old imperial capital Hué. After the news that Hanoi was in the hands of the Vietminh reached Hué, this government, which counted among its members several prominent non-Communist nationalists, decided on August 22 to resign. Not surprisingly, this was interpreted by most Vietnamese, of whom very few knew the exact political nature of the Vietminh, as a delib-erate step to make room for the regime that was centered in Hanoi. In this assumption the Vietnamese people were emphatically con-firmed when Bao Dai, the last hereditary Emperor of Vietnam, resigned on August 25, 1945, with an unmistakable expression of support for the Hanoi regime under Ho Chi Minh.

No less important was what happened in Saigon. There the Communists, still lacking the strength they had in Hanoi, felt ob-liged to share power, in a "Provisional Executive Committee for the South," with the religious-political sects, the Saigon Trotskyites, and several minor nationalist groups. Nothing proves more convinc-ingly that the Vietminh was also popular in Saigon than the decision of this joint committee, taken on August 25, 1945, to place itself under the authority of Hanoi. No nationalist in the South had, at this time, the courage openly to oppose the Hanoi regime.

As Harold Isaacs put it in his *No Peace for Asia:* "The Vietminh *was* [by August 25, 1945] solidly in power in the north and south." And in a chronological survey of antecedents of the

Vietnamese war, the *New York Times* of January 28, 1973 wound up the year 1945 by stating: "The Vietminh led by Ho Chi Minh take control of Vietnam."

All of which raises the very important question why the Vietnamese Communists achieved what no ruling European Communist party can claim: power through popular support, instead of through terror or Russian military presence.

In one of my first meetings with Ngo Dinh Diem at the end of October 1954 I asked him why the Communists in Vietnam were so much stronger than in any other country I knew of. (At least in his private talks with me, Diem never denied that Ho Chi Minh had achieved control of the whole country by the end of August 1945.) I found Diem's answer, which I was able to confirm in all my later studies, immediately convincing: The unusual strength of Vietnamese Communism resulted from the social, political and economic policies of the colonial regime. No democratic movements had been permitted by the French, and in underground work the Communists were superior to all other groups; no indigenous property-owning middle-class, which would have rejected Communism, was allowed to develop; all modern sectors of the economy were in French hands. Capitalism, as far as it existed in Vietnam, was foreign, which meant that anti-colonialism easily became also anti-capitalism, of which the Communists were the most determined exponents. (I shall never forget the remark Diem made in this context: "We Vietnamese nationalists are all some kind of socialists.")

To these reasons for the strength of Vietnamese Communism, which has so far not been matched by any other Communist party, must be added the political genius of Ho Chi Minh. Not only was he able to adapt a doctrine born in the industrialized West to the needs of an Asian nation of peasants. Still more important was his ability to convince the people that as a nationalist he was second to no one, and that true national independence could be achieved only under the leadership of the Vietminh.

II.
Whose Aggression?

Anyone who knows that in August 1945 the Communists had become masters of the whole country will have no trouble in seeing that Hanoi's involvement in the struggle first to maintain and later to regain control of the country's south was neither aggression nor foreign interference in the affairs of another country.

Aggression there was already in Vietnam in 1945, and it was definitely foreign. But it was not aggression by the Communist North against a non-Communist South, which, if it had occurred at all in 1945, would certainly not have been "foreign." Why should the Communists have attacked the South whose leaders by the end of August had recognized the authority of the Hanoi regime? Aggression in Vietnam, directed not against Communism but against the country's newly acquired independence, began with the attempt of the French to reconquer, in a war that lasted almost nine years, their best Indochinese colony. This colony France had lost, first to the Japanese, and, after the surrender of the Japanese, to the Communist-led Vietnamese movement of national liberation.

The first act of French aggression took place only a few days after the British army of occupation in the southern half of Vietnam had freed and rearmed French army units which the Japanese had interned in March 1945. French military action, which aimed at reestablishing colonial rule, started with an attack on the new local administration in Saigon on September 23, 1945, exactly four weeks after Emperor Bao Dai had resigned in favor of Ho Chi Minh and the Provisional Executive Committee for the South had aligned itself with Hanoi.

The aim of the French who at this time had not yet begun to talk about stopping Communism, was made clear by General Jean Leclerc, who, on September 30, 1945, stated in Saigon: "I did not come back to Indochina to give Indochina back to the Indochinese."

When the French, after five months of brutal warfare against Vietnamese resistance, still had not achieved full control of the South, they recognized that they lacked the military strength for an

immediate extension of the war to the Center and North of the
country. This, and the fact that they could not attack the North as
long as the Chinese Nationalist army was there, prompted Paris to
rely temporarily on diplomacy in its scheme to conquer the whole of
Vietnam. On March 6, 1946, the French concluded an agreement
with Ho Chi Minh, recognizing not only his government but also
Vietnam as a "free state" within the French Union. The French also
agreed to elections in the South for the reunification of the country,
and even promised to retire altogether from Vietnam within five
years. Because of these promises and also because the French, in a
treaty with Chiang Kai-shek, had succeeded in getting the Chinese
army of occupation to leave Vietnam, Hanoi agreed to let the French
bring 15,000 of their troops into the part of Vietnam still under firm
Communist control.

That the French had no intention of living up to any part of this
agreement Ho Chi Minh found out only a few weeks later, when the
de Gaulle-appointed High Commissioner for Indochina, Thierry
d'Argenlieu, stated publicly in Saigon that French rule over all of
Indochina could be established only by force. And instead of letting
the people of the South decide, through the agreed-upon election,
whether they wished to be reunited with the North, d'Argenlieu
proclaimed Cochinchina (as the South of Vietnam was then called)
on June 1, 1946, a French-controlled separate state.

But not until November 1946 did the French feel strong
enough—behind a screen of lies about events in the port-city of
Haiphong—to start military action against the North. An incident
over customs control, which the French tried to take away from the
Hanoi government, served as a pretext for extending the war to the
North. On November 23, 1946, the French killed, according to their
own admission, over six thousand civilians in Haiphong. In an order
to the French general in Haiphong, his Commander-in-Chief in
Saigon, General Valluy, said on November 22: "Use all the means at
your disposal to make yourself complete master of Haiphong and so
bring the Vietnamese Army around to a better understanding of the
situation."

Less than four weeks later, the French were ready to take deci-

sive action in Hanoi as well. On December 19 they issued an ul-
timatum demanding that the Vietminh government dissolve its
para-military and police forces and let the French army assume
control of the capital. Recognizing this as a declaration of war which
left him only the choice of resistance or capitulation, Ho Chi Minh
acted more as a nationalist than a Communist when he called on his
people to defend Vietnamese national independence against the attempt of the French to extend colonial rule by force also over North
Vietnam.

According to French propaganda, this decision of the Vietminh
leadership was the beginning of the first Indochina war. The truth,
however, is that in December 1946, this war had already been going
on for fifteen months—ever since the French, on September 23,
1945, had attacked and eliminated the local Vietnamese authorities
in Saigon, thus starting what for the unfortunate people of Vietnam
became a modern "Thirty Years War."

The Vietnamese resistance against unprovoked French military
intervention was soon denounced in the West as "Communist aggression." What may be hard to explain to a new generation of
young Americans is the fact that their own country, in spite of its
claim to an anti-colonial foreign policy, accepted this lie. In any
case, Washington decided, as early as May 1950, that the United
States must support the French in Indochina.

It was of course not easy to justify this policy before the American people and the "free world." American public opinion might
well have rejected it if the people had been less ignorant about
political conditions in Indochina at the end of World War II, and
had been told truthfully how the fighting had started. It required a
tidal wave of falsehood to persuade Americans into accepting the
myth that not French, but Communist, aggression was responsible
for the first Indochina war.

One of these lies, after 1950, was to present the Vietnamese
Communists as being mere agents of Red China. The great mass of
our people, uninformed about contemporary Asian history, was
then led to conclude that without Communist China there would

never have been an Indochina war. This conclusion could of course
be drawn only if one were ignorant of the historical fact that
Vietnam had been Communist and the Indochina war had broken
out fully four years *before* the victory of Communism in China.

As if our leaders were preparing for the even more difficult task
of justifying direct American military intervention, they began to
justify their support for the French with a new argument. Thanks to
this support, America was told, "Communist aggression has been
checked." So said Secretary of State Dean Acheson at a press conference on June 18, 1952. Acheson added that "once again the policy
of meeting aggression with force is paying off," and now, in retrospect, one is inclined to think he must have been possessed by an evil
spirit. To say in 1952 that Communism had been checked in Indochina makes it rather difficult for the advocates of this policy to
explain today how the victory of Communism in Vietnam came
about twenty-three years later—which may be one reason we are
now being asked to "put Vietnam behind us."

III.
The Beginning of U. S. Involvement

Opponents of American policy in Vietnam have frequently argued
against the notion that United States involvement in the struggle for
Indochina began only under President Eisenhower and after the
Geneva Agreement of July 21, 1954. They correctly pointed out
that Washington had been deeply involved since May 1950, when
President Truman and Secretary of State Acheson decided that
Washington must support the French in Indochina, under the pre-
text that it was a war against Communist aggression.

This decision was an important step on the road to increasing
American involvement, but it was by no means its beginning. The
true beginning must be dated back another five years—to the encounter between Truman and Churchill at the Potsdam Conference
of July 1945. Well aware that President Franklin D. Roosevelt had
been opposed to a French return to Indochina, Churchill was now as
eager as the French themselves to convince President Truman that

America's Western allies must not be forced to give up their colonies. Churchill succeeded, largely—as Harold Isaacs put it—thanks to Truman's "ignorance and indifference."

"In a world boiling with nationalist fervor in the wake of World War II" says the Vietnamese nationalist Dong Duc Khoi, "the Americans chose to back the French effort to reconquer their Indochinese colony."

It is no idle speculation to assume that if Roosevelt had still been alive in July 1945 the French would never have returned to Indochina with American approval, let alone American help. The First Indochina war would then never have taken place, and without the First there would certainly never have been a Second Indochina war. But long before the United States financed 78 per cent of the cost of the French Indochina war in 1953/54, their war had to some extent also become America's war.

IV.
The United States and Ho Chi Minh

If Truman had been only a little less ignorant of what had happened in Vietnam before and after August 1945, he might well have argued, as the shrewd politician he was, not only that America had nothing to gain by helping the French return to Indochina but that it had nothing to lose if it recognized and even supported an independent Vietnam under Ho Chi Minh. After all, in fighting the Japanese in Vietnam, Ho Chi Minh had for several months before the end of the war been regarded by well-informed Americans in Southern China—officers of the OSS and even the American Commander in Kunming, General Chennault—as some sort of an ally. Because supporting Ho was in the interest of the American military in China, repeated warnings by the French and by nationalist Chinese that this meant supporting Vietnamese Communism were disregarded. (On this little known episode see my review in the Summer 1974 issue of *Dissent* of the revealing book *Ho Chi Minh: A Biographical Introduction*, by Charles Fenn.)

Now that all efforts have failed to prevent Vietnam from becoming again what it already was thirty years ago—a Communist country—the question of what our relations to Vietnam should be will doubtless soon become the subject of a national debate. Today it is easy to show that Truman's decision to support the return of the French to Indochina was catastrophic for all the peoples and countries involved. While it must today be obvious to every thinking person that this course of action was profoundly mistaken, it is not so easy to see that the opposite policy—recognition of Ho Chi Minh's Vietnam after 1945—would have made good sense for the United States. To reach this conclusion, however, requires some knowledge of Vietnamese history, ancient as well as modern.

That the Communists wanted such recognition is clear even apart from the fact that Ho Chi Minh almost begged for it in several letters to President Truman. (One of these letters, highly convincing, was recently published by Clyde Edwin Pettit in his book *The Experts.*)

Whatever chances Ho Chi Minh had, if not actually to prevent the French from attacking his regime, then at least to deny them American support, depended entirely on recognition of his regime by the United States. A statement by the Strategic Services Unit, War Department, of March 27, 1946, shows that some Americans were well aware of this: "Ho Chi Minh is firmly convinced that what his country needs most in the struggle for independence is the sympathy and understanding of the American people." (See *The Experts*, p. 26)

The chief reason it would have made sense for the United States to pursue such a policy is not only that in the struggle for control of Indochina "there was never a serious American interest involved" (Geoffrey Barraclough). Equally important is the effect on the political evolution of Vietnamese Communism that could reasonably have been expected from American recognition of Ho's regime. As James Wechsler put it in *The New York Post* of April 22, 1975: "In retrospect there are many who believe a wiser more sophisticated U.S. policy toward Ho Chi Minh could have paved the way for a kind of neutralist, Titoist Vietnam and averted much of the tragedy of the last two decades." (For the Vietnamese people it was three decades.)

Without having any illusions about Vietnamese Communists, I would go even farther and say that for compelling historical reasons Ho Chi Minh would very likely have become a better "Titoist" than Tito himself. In becoming Communist in 1945, Vietnam neither received nor needed any kind of help from far-away Russia. Historical circumstances peculiar to Vietnam and utterly different from those that produced the satellites of Eastern Europe created the first Communist country which, unless subject to foreign aggression, did not depend for its survival on the power of the Soviet Union.

Even more important is something which in America is still not sufficiently recognized as a highly distinctive feature of Vietnamese nationalism. As a result of more than two thousand years of struggle against Chinese rule and efforts to re-annex their country, the Vietnamese people have never lost their deep-rooted fear of once again being dominated by their big northern neighbor. For all Vietnamese, Communists and anti-Communists alike, it was self-evident in 1945 that true independence required not only an end to French colonial rule but also a foreign policy directed, under all historical circumstances, toward keeping Vietnam independent of China.

No one knew better than Ho Chi Minh himself that one of the main reasons for his political success had been his ability to convince most Vietnamese that he was at least as good a nationalist as any of the Vietnamese leaders opposed to the Vietminh, many of whom had at one time or another betrayed the cause of national independence by collaborating with the colonial regime. Proud of having achieved power without either Russian or Chinese support, Ho Chi Minh was as little inclined to become an underling of either Stalin or Mao Tse-tung as the Vietnamese people were to submit again to foreign rule.

For all these reasons, as well as because American pressure might have forced the French to retire from Indochina as early as 1946, it is more than likely that a man of Ho's political adaptability would, if Truman had responded to his appeals, have made Vietnam the first

Communist country to have friendly relations with the United States.

Not Ho Chi Minh's choice, but our misguided policy, forced Ho, in order to continue Vietnamese resistance to the French, to accept a certain degree of dependence on Russia. After 1950 that dependance was extended to Communist China. Yet this never led Ho to ask for or accept Russian or Chinese soldiers on Vietnamese soil. Russian and Chinese military aid remained limited to the delivery of arms, which only the resolve of the Vietminh fighters and the support of large numbers of the people made effective—a decisive political aspect of the struggle which was consistently underestimated first by the French and later even more by most Americans.

V.
The U. S. and Vietnam up to 1954

Despite an army which by summer 1951 had been built up to a strength of 391,000 men, the French suffered a string of defeats culminating in Dien Bien Phu in early May 1954. They had now reached the point when the collapse of their efforts to regain Vietnam by force was only a question of time.

But, unlike most of their countrymen, long disgusted with the "dirty war," France's civilian and military leaders were still unable to face, let alone publicly admit, this unpleasant truth. For more than seven years they had hardly ever mentioned Vietnam without confidently predicting that their victory was not only certain, but even imminent. As early as March 1947, the Minister of Defense Paul Corte-Floret said, and probably believed, that "there is no longer a military problem in Indochina." And when this problem seven years later had become really serious for the French, Foreign Minister Georges Bidault stated, exactly two months before the fall of Dien Bien Phu: "Ho Chi Minh is about to capitulate." Less than one hundred days after their own capitulation at Dien Bien Phu, the French, by signing the Geneva Agreement on the Cessation of Hostilities in Viet-Nam, admitted that their war against Ho Chi Minh could not be won. The First Indochina war was over.

The military failure of the French should have proved to any politically mature American that the decision of the French, under de Gaulle's leadership, to return to Indochina after the end of World War II had been an enormous mistake. But why, historians will long continue to ask, did America's political leadership not draw the logical conclusion that support of this war of colonial reconquest had been mistaken? And why, instead of taking the retreat of the French as a welcome opportunity to put an end to America's involvement, did Washington embark on a course of ever-increasing involvement, which eventually led to the second Indochina war?

An American decision in 1954 to leave Indochina to the Indochinese would of course have been an admission that U. S. support for the French had been a mistake from the very beginning—something which most of our leaders even today, after the total failure of U. S. intervention in Indochina, refuse to admit.

At this point it is important to realize the extent to which the French Indochina war had become, long before 1954, also an American war—no longer a war to give Indochina back to the French but to stop "Communist aggression." As early as May 1951, according to President Truman, France was no longer waging a colonial war, but merely helping the already free people of Indochina to defeat Communism. Truman made the following amazing statement: "The Communist assault in Indochina has been checked by the free people of Indochina with the help of the French."

The myth that the war the French had started in September 1945 was caused by Communist aggression was propagated in the United States not only by the President and the Secretary of State; Congress too subscribed to it and until the spring of 1954, was almost unanimous in approving support of the French. Congressman John F. Kennedy, for instance, (who, however, had enough political sense and courage to revise his position after 1950) said in a speech in January 1949: "The House must now assume the responsibility of preventing the onrushing tide of Communism from engulfing all Asia." And Senator Mike Mansfield, not only supporting aid to the French but also sharing, like Truman, their optimism about the outcome of the struggle, said in October 1953: "The Vietminh can be turned back if U. S. military aid is continued."

As the position of the French became more and more difficult, American expressions of optimism about the outcome of the first Indochina war began to emphasize that the predicted victory of the French depended on an increase of U. S. military aid. Even a man like Admiral W. Radford, who as Chairman of the Joint Chiefs of Staff opposed the sending of American troops to Indochina, stated on March 22, 1954: "The French are going to win. It is a fight that is going to be finished with our help."

The extent to which American aid to the French had already become direct military intervention was revealed in another speech (on February 8, 1954) by Senator Mansfield who said: "I fully approve the sending of additional B-26 bombers. I am glad that 25 C-47s were sent last December. I see nothing wrong in sending 200 technicians to assist the 125 technicians who have been there working under the Military Assistance Advisory group . . . I think that is good sound policy."

But neither this kind of military involvement nor the fact— unknown to most Americans—that the United States was already paying nearly 80 per cent of what the war cost, can explain the degree to which public opinion had begun to accept the idea that a victory of the French in Indochina was a vital interest of the United States. This acceptance was the result of propaganda conducted for years by the country's political leaders, newspapers, magazines, radio and television. In disregard of historical fact, this propaganda described the Indochina war not as a struggle between colonialism and Indochinese national aspirations (which it was in spite of Communist leadership), but exclusively as a war between international Communism and the "free world."

Indeed, once the American people had been persuaded that a French loss of Indochina would be a defeat of the "free world," it seemed logical to conclude that the defeat of the French would also be an American defeat. But America, of course, cannot and must never be defeated, reason enough why we had to help the French. Knowing that the only foreign power in Indochina was France, it would be hard for future American students of Asian history to understand how intelligent Americans could ever have taken seriously French statements such as one made by General Maurice Dejean, French Commissioner General, who said in Hanoi on November 4, 1953: "We shall never abandon the Indochinese peninsula to a foreign power." No Frenchman, however, was stupid enough to go as far as Dean Acheson did in a State Department Bulletin of February 13, 1950, when he called Ho Chi Minh, widely recognized even by his opponents as the personification of Vietnamese anti-colonialism, "the mortal enemy of native independence."

The course the United States was likely to take in the struggle for Indochina once the French had to give it up could be predicted with a high degree of accuracy when President Eisenhower, at a news conference five days after the fall of Dien Bien Phu, stated: "I don't think the free world ought to write off Indochina." This of course implied what Senator W. F. Knowland said some three weeks later: "The United States should face up to the fact that it may have to fight in Indochina."

VI.
The U. S. and The Geneva Agreements

It seems that historians of U. S. involvement in Indochina have overlooked the fact that at least one influential American foresaw that a negotiated settlement of the first Indochina war would give victory to the Communists. This man was Vice President Richard M. Nixon. As early as November 4, 1953, at a dinner given in his honor by the French High Commissioner in Hanoi, Nixon stated: "The U. S. would vigorously disapprove of any negotiations for peace in Indochina."

In order to make such negotiations unnecessary Nixon, when he saw that the often-prophesized victory of the French was no longer certain, began to agitate for greater and more direct U. S. military support of the French. In a speech before the Society of Newspaper Editors on April 6, 1954, he said that the French could still win; but since they needed more men, which France, tired of the war, will not supply, "the Administration must face up to the situation and dispatch forces." Two days later, at a meeting in Cincinnati, Ohio, he spoke as if sending "our boys" to fight in Indochina was the only way of preventing an "outright surrender to the Communists."

However, between the fall of Dien Bien Phu and the conclusion of the Geneva Agreement not only Congress—encouraged by Churchill's opposition to any allied intervention in Indochina—but also President Eisenhower, Secretary of State John Foster Dulles and important military leaders were still against the dispatch of American forces to rescue the French. (Churchill had recognized, as de Gaulle did somewhat later, that continued military intervention was not the right way of fighting Communism in Indochina.) On July 19, 1954, two days before the French signed what Nixon must have regarded as a surrender to the Communists, Dulles said that the U. S., although not signing any agreement at Geneva, "will not do anything to upset any reasonable accord sought by the French." Dulles must already have known that apart from the cease-fire agreement between the French and the Vietminh, nothing else agreed upon at Geneva would have to be signed by any of the powers participating in the conference.

Far from creating two separate Vietnamese countries, the portion of the Geneva Agreements signed by the French and the Vietminh clearly stated that the country would merely be temporarily divided into two military zones. All-Vietnamese elections would bring about the reunification of the country. It was the certainty that they would win these elections, set for July 1956, which induced the Communists, although close to total military victory, to accept this compromise solution to end the war.

That they would indeed win these elections every knowledgeable Frenchman, American and Vietnamese took for granted. *Time* magazine of November 22, 1954, for instance, told its many readers that "as of today, the winner would be Ho Chi Minh." Leo Cherne, Chairman of the International Rescue Committee, whose concern with Vietnam preceded that of most Americans, wrote in *Look* magazine of January 25, 1955: "If elections were held today, the

overwhelming majority of the Vietnamese would vote Communist."
(Even as late as August 1, 1965, Senator Richard B. Russell, Demo-
crat of Georgia and Chairman of the Senate Armed Services Com-
mittee, who doubted the wisdom of sending American troops to
Indochina, said on C.B.S. *Face the Nation* that "probably 75% of all
South Vietnamese would vote for Uncle Ho if given the chance.")

It is easy enough to see why the French, no longer confident that
they could win this long, unpopular war, accepted a solution which
promised to make the whole of Vietnam again what it had been in
September 1945. But if the Geneva Agreement confirmed Nixon's
prediction that a negotiated settlement would mean a Communist
victory, why did the United States not immediately oppose the
Geneva settlement? That it did not is evident from a statement of the
chief delegate, Bedell Smith, at the close of the conference (repeating
what Dulles had said on July 19) that the United States, although no
party to the agreement, would do nothing to upset it, either by the
threat or use of force.

In spite of this statement, it soon become clear that Washington
had accepted the Geneva settlement with two reservations, both
incompatible with a correct interpretation of the agreement. One
was to regard the seventeenth parallel, not, as stated in the cease-fire
treaty, as a temporary dividing line between two military zones, but
rather as a permanent border between two separate states—North
and South Vietnam. The second—a logical consequence of the
first—was to disregard the Final Declaration and the projected
reunification of the country by opposing the elections scheduled for
July 1956—the chief reason why the Communists had agreed to the
cease-fire.

I do not believe that the United States ever really intended to
remove Communism from North Vietnam, or that our leaders already knew in July 1954 that America would have to go to war in
order to "save" the half of Vietnam not yet under Communist control after July 1954. What they expected was the evolution, with
American economic and military aid, of a viable, anti-Communist
and pro-American regime in South Vietnam.

The chief reason for this expectation was already hinted at by President Eisenhower in a message to Winston Churchill in April 1954. France, he said, must grant "unequivocal independence" to Vietnam, "so that American entry into Indochina would not have the taint of colonialism." This was an indirect admission that the U.S.-supported first Indochina war was—if not exclusively, at least largely—a war of colonial reconquest. This was confirmed even by Secretary of State Dulles, who, as quoted by Emmett John Hughes in his *Ordeal of Power*, stated still more explicitly than Eisenhower: "We have a clean base there [in Indochina] now without a taint of colonialism. Dien Bien Phu was a blessing in disguise."

But if "a taint of colonialism" was the reason America could not come to the rescue of the French after Dien Bien Phu, would this not lead many Americans to conclude that support of the French in Indochina had also been tainted by colonialism?

Anti-colonialism, which could not be mentioned as long as the U. S., between 1945 and 1954, supported the French in Indochina, was now revived in order to justify American policy in Indochina after the French were no longer there. Indirectly admitting that America had supported a colonial war was a small risk compared to the advantages American propaganda gained by emphasizing that this was henceforth no longer the case. With the "taint of colonialism" removed, American policy was now supporting an anti-Communist South Vietnam which by definition was a "free" country, and as such—no matter what kind of regime developed in Saigon—part of the "free world." In the eyes of most Americans this justified "President Eisenhower's decision to take no notice of the Geneva agreement" (J. M. Cameron). Even if sabotage of the scheduled elections should involve the United States in another war, it could now be convincingly presented to the American people as a war in defense of freedom.

A really free and democratic South Vietnam, willing to accept a state of peaceful co-existence with the Communist North, was not of course an automatic result of the withdrawal of the French from Indochina. But efforts to create it would certainly have deserved whatever support the United States was able to supply. Today, however, it is becoming clear that there was never any true freedom for us to defend in South Vietnam, neither after 1954 under Ngo Dinh Diem nor at any time up to or during the nearly eight years of brutal dictatorship under Nguyen Van Thieu. The time may also not be far off when a majority of our people will recognize that no real American interest would have been affected if the elections of 1956 had been held and Ho Chi Minh, instead of Diem, had become the legitimate ruler in Saigon.

Future historians may very likely regard the claims that in South Vietnam the United States was defending a free country against foreign aggression among the great political lies of this century. To regard as foreign any Vietnamese who moved from the North into the South, either to flee from Communism or to fight for it, leads to the absurd conclusion that the more than half a million Catholics who moved South after the Geneva agreement should have been treated by the Saigon regime as foreigners. Let us remember that the only foreigners who fought in Vietnam were the French during the First and the Americans (with some so-called allies) during the Second Indochina war.

VII.
The United States and Diem

It is one of the legends of contemporary Vietnamese history propagated not only by the Communists but also by the French, that Ngo Dinh Diem was America's choice to head the first government of South Vietnam. This legend is based largely on the expressions of satisfaction with which his appointment was greeted by some leading Americans acquainted with Diem, such as Cardinal Spellman, Senator Mike Mansfield, Justice William Douglas, and Representative Thomas Dodd. The truth is that neither President Eisenhower nor Secretary Dulles was consulted before Bao Dai, the former Emperor and so-called Head of State under the French after 1949, appointed Diem on June 6, 1954. With the consent of his former French masters, Bao Dai decided it would be wise to replace a government of discredited war-time collaborators with one headed by an anti-Communist known also as an opponent of colonialism. No doubt Bao Dai and the French were hoping that as a spokesman of Vietnamese national independence, Diem might be able to compete with Ho Chi Minh. Until early May 1955, when Diem consolidated his power by defeating an armed uprising of one of the so-called sects that had collaborated with the French, Washington's attitude toward him could be described only as lukewarm. I became aware of this when, after January 1955, I was trying to get Washington to strengthen its support of Diem. Only after May 1, 1955 did Washington become convinced that Diem would be able to gain popular support for an anti-Communist regime in Saigon, and that he was also determined to prevent a Communist take-over of the South either through the 1956 elections or by force.

Diem now began to be celebrated in countless statements by influential Americans as one of the great heroes of the "free world," who would insure the survival of a non-Communist South Vietnam. The fact that his regime developed into a police state, denying the people all essential political freedoms, did nothing for many years to dampen official American enthusiasm.

Our government and other American admirers of Diem cannot have been unaware of the evidence which by the end of 1959 proved that his regime had developed all the attributes of a brutal dictatorship. As early as November 1955, the well-informed historian Bernard Fall began to warn against this trend. About the elections of October 1955, through which Bao Dai was ousted as Chief of State and Diem was made President, Fall told any official willing to listen what he wrote later in his book *The Two Vietnams:* "There is no doubt that this plebiscite was only a shade less fraudulent than most electoral tests under a dictatorship." When the prominent anti-Communist Dr. Phan Quang Dan gained a solid majority in the 1959 National Assembly elections against a pro-Diem candidate in a Saigon area where the elections could not be manipulated as they were in the rest of the country, Dan was not allowed to take his seat and a little later was even sent to a so-called re-education camp. As I wrote in my 1972 book on Vietnam *A Dragon Defiant:* "The highly political intellectual elite was incensed by the denial of basic civil liberties and the arrest of anyone who dared openly to criticize the regime, often men of known anti-Communist convictions" (p. 94). In *The Lost Revolution* (1965), Robert Shaplen, one of the best-informed critics of the Diem regime, wrote: "Diem and [his brother] Nhu came to ignore the constitution completely and acted by decree and by personal—and often private—orders to underlings all the way down to the village level."

It is impossible to believe that nobody in Washington read the South Vietnam law of May 6, 1959, which extended the death sentence for acts against the security of the state to the mere spreading of rumors. It reads as follows: "Anyone who intentionally proclaims or spreads by any means unauthorized news about prices or rumors contrary to truth or distorts truth concerning the present or future situation in the country or abroad . . . will be sentenced to death."

Much earlier, in June 1956, Diem had suppressed a modest pre-colonial element of democracy—election of village and municipal councils—which even the colonial regime had respected. Such anti-democratic measures opened the eyes of at least some American officials. An intelligence report from Saigon of May 1959 stated: "A facade of representative government is maintained but the government is in fact authoritarian." Of this, Vice President Johnson could hardly have remained unaware during his visit to Saigon in May, 1961. He must have decided that to admit this truth would have made it too difficult to continue American support for the Diem regime. Or is it possible that he really believed what he said when he put Diem "in the vanguard of those leaders who stand for freedom"?

One might still find excuses for Senator John F. Kennedy since it was five years earlier that he found South Vietnam's "political liberty an inspiration" (in a speech before a Washington meeting of the American Friends of Vietnam on June 1, 1956—an occasion where I too still spoke in defense of the Diem regime). President Eisenhower too, on September 20, 1956, felt he could still "point with pride to the free nation of Vietnam," a statement topped only by Mayor Robert Wagner, who during Diem's visit in New York in May 1957 called him "a man to whom freedom is the very breath of life." But what will forever be truly shocking to any future student of American attitudes toward South Vietnam is the fact that similar statements were still made even after members of the House Foreign Affairs Committee, returning from a study mission in Vietnam, reported on May 22, 1962: "Since President Diem assumed office in 1955 he has taken dictatorial control, either directly or through a small group of intimates, many of whom are members of his family." And as an illustration of what this meant for non-Communists opposed to Diem's dictatorship, they added: "It is estimated some 30,000 South Vietnamese nationalists are in concentration camps."

Praising a dictator by calling him a man devoted to freedom was from the very beginning of Diem's rule combined with expressions of optimism as regards the chances for survival of a non-Communist South Vietnam. This was frequently presented not as a future likelihood but a goal already achieved. I do not take seriously someone like Joseph F. Flannelly, at the time auxiliary bishop of New York, who on May 12, 1957, said in the presence of Diem in St. Patrick's Cathedral that "this God-fearing anti-Communist and courageous statesman has saved Vietnam." More important, because more likely to be taken as a statement of fact, was President Eisenhower's remark on May 20, 1957, that "Vietnam has been saved for freedom."

In light of what eventually became of South Vietnam, it is not easy to explain the optimism to which most American political and military leaders subscribed for so many years. Ignorance of Vietnamese history and misinterpretation of the little they knew about it certainly did not help to overcome the profound misconceptions on which our Vietnam policy was based. But while this helps one to understand America's original involvement in the struggle for Indochina, it takes more to teach us why our leaders failed to learn from experience that their aims, although pursued with inhumane means, remained unattainable.

Once a country or political movement has embarked on an unrealistic course of action, the efforts of its leaders to justify what they are doing are likely to produce a kind of political self-deception, proving that the first victims of propaganda are usually its authors.

We have plenty of evidence for this rather common affliction among politicians and military leaders, which in regard to Vietnam reached epidemic proportions, especially after 1965. Just before and several weeks after November 2, 1963, when a group of generals, with American approval, put an end to the rule of Ngo Dinh Diem, a new wave of optimistic statements was launched that the Communist-led insurrection against the Saigon regime was about to be defeated. On October 31, 1963, General Paul D. Harkins, head of the U. S. Assistance Command in Saigon, said in an interview in Tokyo that "the end of the war was in sight." Therefore, a reduction in the number of American military advisers "can now begin." On the same day, President Kennedy too expressed the hope that the number of these advisers, which had already reached 16,500, might soon be reduced to 1,000. At a news conference on November 14, he said "we are bringing back several hundred before the end of the year." The same promise was made by Secretary of Defense Robert S. McNamara on November 19.

I do not doubt that these men really intended to do what they announced, but none of them ever explained later why the number of these advisers, far from being reduced after November 1963, was increased to 23,000 during 1964.

Supporting the overthrow of Diem was no doubt an important decision in the evolution of Washington's Vietnam policy, although it failed to change this policy in any significant way. I was among those who took President Kennedy's obvious wish to have Diem replaced as a sign that he had begun to question the policy of trying to save South Vietnam by killing Communists and maintaining a socially and politically reactionary dictatorship. Killing Communists I had long recognized as a sure way to increase Communist strength in Vietnam, although I did not yet know what Charles de Gaulle had written on this subject in a letter to Kennedy on May 31, 1961. De Gaulle, who had obviously grown convinced that he had been wrong on insisting that Indochina remain a French colony after World War II, said in this letter: "The more you commit yourself [in Indochina] against Communism, the more Communists will appear to be champions of National independence."

No one will ever know what American policy toward Vietnam might have become if Kennedy had not been assassinated soon after the fall and murder of Diem. His support of Diem's policy, although not irreversible after the fall of Diem, was certainly a first step leading to the Second Indochina war. But it was Lyndon Johnson who, in the time between November 1963 and February 1965, made the Second Indochina war a certainty.

VIII.
My Own Involvement

What follows here is an attempt to explain how a democratic Socialist could get involved as deeply as I did, with the policy the United States pursued in Vietnam soon after the Geneva Conference and even become for several years active in support of the Diem regime.

Being involved, however, did not mean—at least in my case— unconditional and continuous support of American policy and the Diem regime. For me it also meant incessant efforts, both in Washington and Saigon, to bring about an awareness of the need for genuine democracy and radical social reforms in South Vietnam. When I recognized that these efforts were bound to fail, especially after the beginning of direct American military intervention, my involvement became that of an open and determined opponent of United States policy in Vietnam.

I want to speak here not only for myself but also for many of my socialist and liberal friends, who, often with strong reservations, shared my views and up to a point supported what I did. Although I shall try to correct a frequently distorted record of my activities in connection with Vietnam, my intention is not to deny that my support of the regime of Ngo Dinh Diem, beyond the first two years was a serious political mistake, for which I, more than any of my friends, must assume responsibility.

My involvement with Vietnam began when the International Rescue Committee asked me in October 1954 to go to Saigon and organize a relief operation for students, intellectuals and orphans

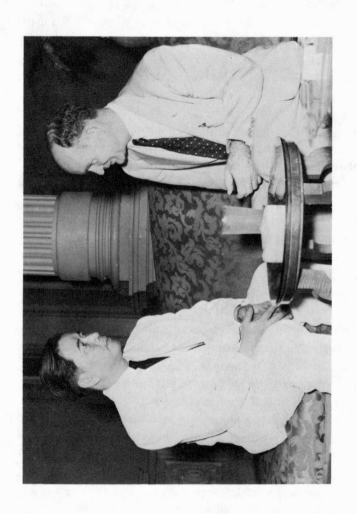

The author with President Ngo Dinh Diem at Independence Palace. (Saigon, December 1954)

The author with the leaders of the refugee students from the University of Hanoi. (Saigon, November 1954)

The author with refugee high school boys and orphans for whom he organized a relief operation. (Saigon, December 1954)

The author translating for President Diem at a press conference in New York, May 1957. To the right of the President, Ambassador Tran Van Chuong.

who, after the end of the First Indochina war, moved from the Communist-controlled North of Vietnam to the South.

The main reason I accepted this assignment was my concern for political refugees—I had been one myself. As a democratic Socialist I also sympathized with people who did not want to live under a Communist regime. I had been engaged in refugee rescue and relief work ever since the annexation of Austria by Hitler-Germany in 1938, helping not only political refugees from fascism but also, after 1945, those from the Communist countries of Eastern Europe. I assumed that people like myself must be among those who left the Communist North of Vietnam—democratic Socialists opposed, for better reasons than most other Vietnamese anti-Communists, to the Hanoi regime.

In this assumption I was not mistaken, as I found out after only a brief time in Saigon. There I met, among refugee students and intellectuals, many firm democrats and Socialists, all happy that with the end of colonialism they could at last disassociate themselves from the Communists, whom as the leading force in the struggle for national independence they had felt obliged to support during the First Indochina war.

Some of my illusions about the possibility of a democratic and socially progressive regime in South Vietnam I acquired in discussions with these non-Communist Vietnamese, who, for reasons that I found plausible, thought that at least for the time being Ngo Dinh Diem was the best hope for their country. That a basis for a viable democratic South Vietnam did not exist but would have to be created, was our common view. What I learned only after years of study and political observation was that the radical social changes this required could not be expected from the small group of traditionally conservative nationalist leaders like Diem. Even when they were uncorrupted and genuine nationalists, these leaders formed only a small urban elite with no political roots among the vast majority of Vietnamese in the country's villages. The Saigon regime—cut off more and more from the rest of the country by its reactionary social policy, and from the politically alert youth and intellectuals by its denial of democracy—never acquired any kind of valid social base. Even before the fall of Diem its supporters consisted almost entirely of corrupt high bureaucrats, the systematically corrupted military and secret service leadership, the small body of landowners and the even smaller American-created group of native war profiteers.

As regards Diem himself, Dong Duc Khoi, one of his early supporters, and later an opponent, wrote in *The New Republic* of May 3, 1975, that Diem was a patriot, but also "a melange of medieval autocracy, of religious fanaticism and total ignorance of the socio-economic imperatives of his nation."

If it took a well-informed, prominent Vietnamese intellectual many years to recognize that Diem must no longer be supported, how could such critical insight be expected from an outsider like myself? Nevertheless, I do not think that I was utterly wrong when, after a brief study of recent Vietnamese history and discussions with democratic Vietnamese opponents of colonialism and Communism, I decided, at the end of 1954, that Diem must be defended.

The chief reason why I became, after my return from Vietnam, what the magazine *Ramparts* of July 1965 called "a one-man lobby for Diem" was simple and compelling. In 1954-55 Diem could be replaced only by a combination of pro-French army leaders and politicians who had collaborated with the colonial regime and thus betrayed the cause of national independence. This would inevitably have prolonged the pre-Geneva conditions under which the people had to choose between accepting continued colonial rule and fighting it in the ranks of the Vietminh. Only a truly anti-colonial regime in the South, headed by a man who had never collaborated with the French, could offer a new choice to the people of South Vietnam. This however would require that the South Vietnamese under such a regime would also see a chance, after the end of colonialism, for a better and freer life than the Communists offered to the people of the North.

This brings me back to the question why the Communists were stronger in Vietnam than in any other country, which in turn raises the even more important question of how the unique strength of the Communist movement affected the prospects for the survival of a

non-Communist South Vietnam. I have treated this question at
some length in one of my articles on Vietnam, published in the
Spring 1965 issue of *Dissent* (and reprinted in the magazine's 20th
Anniversary issue of Spring 1974). Much of what I wrote in this
article I had told Diem in discussion with him during my first stay in
Saigon. If, as I put it, Communism in Vietnam is the heritage of
colonialism, Ho Chi Minh's hold on the people can be weakened
only by a Saigon regime determined to liquidate all economic, social
and political remnants of colonialism. It was more urgent than anything else, I argued, to put an end to the ruthless exploitation by
large landowners, money lenders and the government of the more
than 80 per cent of the people, tenants or poor peasants, who had
supported the Communists more out of despair than political conviction.

To gain popular support for a non-Communist South Vietnam, I
told Diem: You must undo the harm the French did that
strengthened the Communists; you must build a socially progressive
society through a radical land-reform and through rapid economic
progress with American aid; and you must let all non-Communist
parties, groups, spokesmen, the politically concerned students and
intellectuals participate in the country's political life.

At this time, even President Eisenhower recognized (but forgot
all too soon) the need for reform. In a letter to Diem of October 23,
1954, offering U. S. aid to South Vietnam, Eisenhower wrote: "The
government of the United States expects that this aid will be met by
performances on the part of the government of Vietnam in undertak-
ing needed reforms." And *The New York Times* of January 8, 1955
reported: "U.S. officials believe that reforms in South Vietnam
could tip the scale in favor of the free world in the all-Vietnamese
elections due in July, 1956."

Instead of making a firm commitment to such a course, Diem in
our talks and his letters to me always found reasons why social and
political reforms could not yet be undertaken. His main argument
was that to undo the damage left by the colonial regime required
time. I agreed with this argument up to early 1956, but had a first
serious disagreement with Diem back in December 1954, when he

said that the need to delay important reform was his chief reason for refusing to participate in the all-Vietnamese elections to be held in July 1956. In order to reduce the possible dangers of the course Diem had decided on in his relations to Hanoi, I made the following suggestion: Propose to Hanoi that these elections be postponed for one or two years and agree to the reunification of the country only if it is accepted, in really free elections, by a majority of the people in the South; but at the same time hold out the prospect of economic cooperation and peaceful coexistence between North and South.

I made this proposal long before I learned that Hanoi had always been ready to discuss a postponement of these elections. But Diem, at least at that time, refused any kind of contact with the leaders of North Vietnam.

To aim at a state of peaceful coexistence with the North would have been correct even if Diem thought it would bring about only a temporary relaxation of tensions. But much worse for the future of South Vietnam than his refusal to talk with Hanoi before July 1956 was his failure to respond to the South's crying need for social and political reforms. His land reform, belatedly undertaken during 1956, was not only woefully inadequate but also effectively sabotaged by the landlords, with the help of their relatives in the administration. Instead of using American aid for an economic crash program to create a measure of prosperity, 80 per cent of the money Diem received was spent for the army, the police and several secret services.

To my letters asking him to grant political freedom to anti-Communist intellectuals, students, Buddhists and any organized non-Communist group, Diem's constant reply was that this would turn out to be of benefit only to the Communists. And to my suggestions that he free certain people who had been put in prison or concentration camps for criticizing his regime, Diem's answer was that these people, if set free, would continue to undermine his regime, and this again would benefit only the Communists.

As early as the summer of 1955, Diem had apparently decided to seek political stability for South Vietnam not through a policy of gaining mass support for his regime but by relying on brutal force.

He sent his army into regions still controlled by the Vietminh. Thousands of Communists, as well as non-Communists sympathizers of the Vietminh, were killed and many more thrown into prisons and concentration camps. All of this happened more than two years before the Communists began to commit acts of terror against local government officials.

Why then did I continue to support Diem after he had chosen, against my continued advice, to seek his regime's survival through terror instead of social, economic and political reforms? The answer to this crucial question sounds hardly believable today. I knew that Diem had begun to imprison some real and suspected Communists, but due to his effective control of all sources of information from the provinces, I remained for several years ignorant of his attempt to defeat Communism by force. Also, during the years he pursued this brutal and politically fatal course, he kept promising me and other concerned liberal Americans that the reforms we were urging on him would soon become law. On October 17, 1955, for instance, he was quoted by *Time* magazine as having said to its correspondent: "I promise you that by the end of this year we will have a democratic regime and national assembly."

When Diem visited the United States in May 1957, I was still far from realizing that behind a pseudo-democratic facade his policy had become the very opposite of what I considered the only justification for American support of a non-Communist regime in Saigon. I agreed to act as one of his political advisers and even wrote three of the speeches he gave during his stay in these United States. But twice during these weeks I had reason to question my respect for Diem's character and my belief in the success of his policies.

One occasion was a New York press conference at which he made me, as his translator from French into English, say what I knew to be a lie—the same lie which President Nguyen Van Thieu told the Pope sixteen years later: that there were no political prisoners in South Vietnam. The other occasion was during a private political discussion I had with Diem in his living quarters in Washington, to which he had asked me to come immediately after his arrival in the United States. Unaware that Diem had already adopted this course more than two years earlier, I warned him against the temptation to fight Communism by killing Communists, instead of pursuing policies that would deprive them of popular support. What I told Diem he ought to have known better than I: if you kill a man known or suspected of being a Communist in a village where almost everybody is a relative of the dead man, you will, if not actually create five new Communists, at least make that many new enemies of your regime.

This I said long before Tran Van Chuong, who had resigned as Diem's ambassador in Washington, called the Diem regime, on the CBS program *Face The Nation* (October 13, 1963), "a government which in fact is simply pushing people into the arms of the Communists." Nor did I know that "even the CIA warned repeatedly that military measures would not work unless accompanied by social reforms instituted by Saigon" (Christopher Lasch).

I was disturbed, but obviously not enlightened, when Diem, instead of answering that he would avoid a course I considered politically disastrous, merely invited me to come to Saigon in order to see what his government's policy could and ought to be.

I had already learned a great deal more about contemporary Vietnamese history by the time of my next encounter with Diem, which took place during my second visit to South Vietnam in August 1958. (My first book on Vietnam, *The Smaller Dragon: A Political History of Vietnam*, had been published in February 1958.) Apart from traveling a good deal and interviewing, as I had done in 1954, many South Vietnamese and American officials, I again had long discussions with Diem, and also with his brother and advisor Nhu. Until August 1958 I had still occasionally defended Diem in public statements, although no longer with the good conscience that had made my efforts in his favor all during 1955 a hopeful political task. This I refused to do after August 1958.

During the next two years, I neither attacked nor publicly endorsed the policy of American support for the Diem regime. The main reason why I felt—in spite of constantly more discouraging news from Saigon—that Diem should still be kept in power, was the mistaken notion that friendly persuasion combined with pressure from Washington, might still induce him to pursue a policy which, at the expense of the Communists, would gain popular support for his regime.

One of the channels through which I tried to pursue this aim was the American Friends of Vietnam, a deeply divided organization which, however, went along, at least as long as I was chairman of its executive committee, with the idea of urging Saigon to adopt more liberal policies. When I became convinced that these efforts were bound to fail and that Diem's socially reactionary and politically represssive regime not only threatened the survival of an independent South Vietnam but even invalidated all arguments in favor of its existence, I began to agitate for the replacement of Diem by a democratic and socially progressive regime. (It still took a long time until I realized that no social basis for such a regime existed in South Vietnam. Not until 1965 did I become convinced that expecting South Vietnam to become a democratic state was an illusion. The forces allied with Western intervention were essentially anti-democratic, and fully aware of the fact that even a minimum of real democracy was incompatible with their desire to remain in power.)

From 1960 on I used every occasion to point out that only a Saigon leadership seeking firm roots among its people could possibly contain the threat of a Communist victory in South Vietnam. But only in 1962 did I become a really active and determined opponent of the Diem regime.

One of my first unequivocal actions in that new role was to write—at the request of a former high official of Diem's government who had been forced into exile—a proclamation for clandestine distribution in South Vietnam, asking the people to join the persecuted democratic leaders in an effort to overthrow the Diem dictatorship.

Soon afterwards, I began to cooperate with former Ambassador Tran Van Chuong in a campaign to convince American public opinion that the main condition for the survival of an independent South Vietnam was to get rid of Diem. I could more easily make this demand than could Ambassador Chuong, who was the father of Diem's powerful sister-in-law Madame Nhu. She, together with her husband, was as much responsible for Diem's failure to weaken the appeal of Communism as Diem himself.

Finally, in June 1963, I called a conference of politically concerned American and Vietnamese social scientists who, after two days of discussion, charged me to produce a memorandum outlining the reasons why an effective policy aiming at saving a non-Communist South Vietnam required the replacement of the Diem regime by a government willing to take such measures as might deprive the Communists of the popular support they still enjoyed.

Soon after I had submitted this memorandum to the State Department, President Kennedy called for a "change of personnel" in the government of South Vietnam, thus signaling to the generals who were conspiring to overthrow Diem that Washington approved of their plot. A cablegram of August 23, 1963, to Henry Cabot Lodge, American Ambassador in Saigon, from the Joint Chiefs of Staff, drafted by Roger Hilsman, Averell Harriman, George W. Ball and Michael V. Forrestal and approved by President Kennedy, made this clear. It reads:

> U. S. government cannot tolerate situation in which power lies in Nhu's hands. Diem must be given a chance to rid himself of Nhu and his coterie and replace them with best military and political personalities available. If, in spite of all your efforts, Diem remains obdurate and refuses, then we must face the possibility that Diem himself cannot be preserved. (See *The Expert*, page 141).

Two facts, however, prevented me from experiencing great satisfaction over the fall of Diem. I did not believe that his replacement by a military government offered much chance for the adoption of the policy of radical reforms I knew was called for; and I was deeply disturbed by the politically unnecessary and despicable murder of Diem and his brother Nhu.

My feeble hopes that a change for the better had occurred survived only a short time. Neither the government headed briefly by General Duong Van Minh nor that of his successor General Nguyen Khanh deviated from the reactionary social policies of Diem. This became evident long before Air Vice-Marshal Nguyen Cao Ky and later General Nguyen Van Thieu assumed dictatorial powers, heading a regime no longer even in need of popular support, since its survival depended henceforth exclusively on the presence, all over South Vietnam, of ever-increasing American military forces.

In concluding this personal part of my book I want to say that I feel no need to apologize for my support, over several years, of a policy aiming at the creation of a socially progressive and democratic South Vietnam. This policy would have offered to at least a part of the Vietnamese people a first chance freely to decide under what kind of regime they wanted to live. Not apologizing, however, does not mean that I minimize, let alone deny, that my support for Diem, although justifiably inspired, was politically mistaken. I have long been convinced that those who fail to recognize their political mistakes will never learn from experience, and that anyone who refuses to admit his mistakes no longer deserves credibility.

Having made this point I want to stress again that since the Spring of 1965 I have attacked United States action and aims in Vietnam. I have done this in public meetings, in radio and TV interviews, in articles published in the U. S. and abroad, and in books on Vietnam.

In view of the frequent distortion of my record, especially by Communist publications, I think I have a right to point out that I spoke up against our Vietnam policy when many others who will be remembered as its opponents were still supporting it, some of them, although with little enthusiasm, until the end of 1966. It may come as a surprise to many readers that this is true even for such prominent critics as Senators J. W. Fulbright, Edward Brooke and to a lesser degree Mike Mansfield, Robert Kennedy and George McGovern. Other prominent Americans who were slow in publicly opposing this policy were Averell Harriman, George F. Kennan and Edwin O. Reischauer, although when they began to speak up, their criticism doubtless became more effective than that of many earlier opponents of what their country was doing in Vietnam.

IX.
A Revealing Correspondence

The following documents, never before published, deal with the early period of my political activities in favor of President Ngo Dinh Diem. My long letter to him of August 1955 and his long reply show how I worked in his favor and how close our personal and political relations were at that time.

The only person to whom I sent a copy of my letter to Diem (reproduced below), was Leo Cherne, who as Chairman of the Board of the International Rescue Committee had persuaded me in October 1954 to go to Vietnam, and whose concern about the conditions for the survival of a non-Communist South Vietnam predated that of most Americans. Here is what Leo Cherne wrote to me about my letter to Diem:

EXECUTIVE DIRECTOR, THE RESEARCH
INSTITUTE OF AMERICA, INC.
DECEMBER 21, 1955

Dear Joe:

This will be just a brief note about your letter to Vietnam. I don't think I have ever read an analysis more penetrating, a criticism with less sting, a set of recommendations with more purpose or an exposition of any character that more completely reveals the stature of the man writing it.

The one thing I would like to know now is whether the person you sent it to ever received it. What concerns me is that he may have and that the absence of an answer reveals something about him.

Thanks very much for showing it to me.

Cordially,
Leo

Apart from our close relationship, this first exchange of letters between Diem and myself also reveals some of the complexities of the political situation in South Vietnam after 1954. What disturbed me greatly were not only the rivalries among the leaders of the various non-Communist nationalist groups, but also the President's apparent inability to deal effectively with the personal and political problems these rivalries created. If I had been more critical of Diem at that time I might have foreseen that under his leadership the

Saigon regime was in danger of developing into a politically ineffective personal dictatorship.

The President's letter, written in French, was five single-spaced pages along. Because of the great length, only the first and last pages of his French are reproduced below. However, I translated it into English, in which it is here reproduced complete. With Diem's permission (obtained through his Embassy in Washington), I sent copies of it to a number of politically interested friends. As an example of their reaction, which was on the whole favorable, I quote Leo Cherne's letter to me about it:

EXECUTIVE DIRECTOR, THE RESEARCH
INSTITUTE OF AMERICA, INC.
JULY 18, 1956

Dear Joe:

I am returning the copy of the letter from President Diem. I have rarely read a more fascinating letter and I wish I had the command of the political forces and personalities that you do so that I could have followed the political developments more completely.

It is clear to me that Diem is entirely sincere in his ideals and convictions. It is not entirely as clear to me that his judgment is as sound, though I am in no position at all to question that judgment.

It would not be the first time that democracy has been lost by one eager to achieve it. I have more than a sneaking suspicion, however, that this is not the case with this man, with this people, at this time. And if that suspicion is so, Joe Buttinger will deserve the lion's share of credit.

Sincerely,
Leo

I did not show the President's letter to any of the Vietnamese who had complained to me about Diem's refusal to activate all existing nationalist groups for the defense of his regime by admitting their leaders to his government. But those to whom I told what the President had written to me about them vigorously denied that there was any truth in Diem's harsh political denunciations, especially in calling some of them fascist and accusing others of being willing to cooperate with the Communists.

Some of these nationalist leaders, for instance Dr. Nguyen Ton Hoan and Dr. Phan Quang Dan whom Diem had singled out as especially dangerous, later showed up as members of several post-Diem Saigon governments, proving that Diem's successors must have considered them reliable anti-Communists.

Most of the others Diem denounced in his letter remained politically unimportant, both before and after the fall of Diem.

Here is my first letter to Diem, written in August of 1955:

Dear Mr. President:

I hope this letter reaches you in the best of health and spirits.

First of all I want to congratulate you on the success your work and your policies have had during the last few months. I have followed your struggle as closely as anyone in the United States and I have always been sure that neither the French nor the rebellious sects would be able to overthrow your government.

Your ambassador in Washington Mr. Tran Van Chuong has probably kept you informed about the activities that have developed around my efforts to work up support for your policies and your government in the United States. You may have seen or heard of the last piece I wrote entitled "An Analysis of the Conflict between United States and French Policies in Vietnam." This piece marks the end of a period in my work for Vietnam. From now on I will have to work in a different manner. Your decision to start a public relations program in the United States is one reason for this. Much of what I have been doing in the way of propaganda and information will now be done by Mr. Oram and his associates. I will continue to support these efforts and advise and help Mr. Oram in every possible way, but my main efforts will go into the project of writing an understandable book on Vietnam for the American public.

Before I retire to the study, however, I should like to express myself, in a personal and confidential manner, on how I see a few aspects of the Vietnamese problem in the context of American foreign policy, and how I regard the chances of American public support for this policy when the inevitable international crisis over Vietnam will be upon us next year.

I am sure you are as much aware as I of the new Communist "peace offensive," and the fact that the present trend of Communist world policy has created new dangers for the preservation of a free Vietnam. The desire to lessen the international tension of the last years has made too many people blind to the dangers contained in the new Communist approach. The election strategy of the Republican party in the United States adds to this danger by presenting President Eisenhower to the nation and to the world as a bringer of peace, as the man who can get somewhere with the Russians, and perhaps even the Chinese. Nobody seems to realize that a price will have to be paid if the present harmony, which is superficial enough, should continue for a while.

If present trends in the international situation continue, the influence of France on United States policy in Vietnam will increase. The French are now very active in the United States in this direction. They even take the trouble to follow my activities, trying to influence or silence me. The French Ambassador and his information service have both been after me for several weeks. They have tried to get the International Rescue Committee to disavow my activities publicly. They know, of course, that they cannot influence me but they try hard enough and sometimes succeed in preventing me from influencing others.

More important I believe is the trend in England. The French are suspect of being an interested party and have lost much credit with the American public as a result of their colonial policies in Indochina and in Africa. The British however are regarded as the possessors of great wisdom in international affairs who, in the case of Vietnam are not motivated by selfish interests and therefore deserved to be listened to. British voices are heard in the American press more and more frequently on the issue of Vietnam, all of them pleading for a policy of compromise which should find expression in your willingness to cooperate in the holding of the elections, arranged for the Vietnamese people by the Chinese and the French in Geneva. To counteract this British propaganda in the United States is of the utmost importance for the success of your policy on the international level. In this respect Mr. Oram and his helpers will face a difficult task. You have made this task easier by accepting the principle of elections for the unification of the country, stipulating at the same time that conditions for free elections must exist before such elections can be held. It would have been a mistake to let the Communists alone proclaim the principle of elections and push you into a purely negative attitude. Your position is of course much more difficult than Ho Chi Minh's. The democratic world has a sentimental attachment to the mere word elections, and it is again the British who, in spite of their reputation as very practical politicians, do not seem to realize that there can be no free elections in an unfree country.

Allow me to make a few additional remarks on this important subject, at the risk of seeming to offer advice which you certainly do not need. In demanding conditions under which elections to unify the country become meaningful, your government has certainly unlimited chances to denounce the Communist regime to the north, but there are also great dangers to this approach. Many people in the United States think that you can ask for conditions which the Communists will have to refuse, thereby demonstrating that they do not want elections which they are not sure to win. These people do not see the danger that Ho Chi Minh might accept all demands which certain naive democrats in the west regard as guarantees for free elections. I think your information services should tell the world what we are trying to say here whenever we have an opportunity: that inspection teams and temporary supervision will not instill confidence in a population exposed to the terror of the regime as soon as the inspection is over; that the Communists can give you permission to print a paper in Hanoi because they have it in their hands to prevent anyone from buying or reading such a paper; that they can also give you permission to hold meetings in the cities of the north because they are in a position to prevent the population from going to such meetings; that conditions for free elections are not to be had by an agreement on paper promising all the liberties existing in free countries; free elections depend on structural changes of the existing regime in the north. If the citizen is not free to move where he wants to in his country, to read, write and speak what he wants to say without having to fear that he will be punished now or later, he can never be free in his voting. A vigorous campaign along these lines should help much in preparing international opinion for the only way out of this election dilemma; namely, to postpone elections for several years *without denouncing the principle of elections for the unification of the country*. In the meantime we have to repeat every day that free elections require a free country, that elections in a totalitarian country are not an act of democracy but a manifestation organized by the government to support the totalitarian regime, and that, therefore, the holding of free elections is only possible after the dissolution of the totalitarian regime. I think part of your strategy should be to hold elections in the south. The Communists will protest. I think they know that they cannot win them. But the west cannot very well oppose such a move on your part. If such elections are not proclaimed as a substitute for those demanded by Geneva, but rather as an internal measure necessary to create a wider democratic basis for your regime, such a move can only further strengthen your position in the democratic world.

Unfortunately, here in the United States we do not only have to counteract the prevailing ignorance and indifference concerning Vietnam, the effects of the Communist peace offensive, the intrigues of the French and the desire of the British to mediate the international conflicts. Increasingly, we have to contend with other opponents, namely personalities and political groups of South Vietnam who are dissatisfied with your course and use every available channel to express their dissatisfaction and to make known their own demands. Up to now I felt completely justified in disregarding the complaints, criticisms and demands of these circles. I had been exposed to much of this while still in Saigon, and although I learned a great deal from some of your critics, all my writings testify to the fact that they had no influence on my positive views of your personality and your political course. In view of the new international situation and the increased presssures we have to expect as we come closer to the Geneva election date, criticism of your policy from these sources will be more effective in the future and can no longer be taken lightly or remain unanswered. A climate will come about in which the pettiest complaints against your policy will find willing ears. The people who agitate against you and your government in the international field will achieve at least one thing: they will create doubts as to the character of your regime and the validity of your democratic intentions. These doubts in turn will weaken the will of the west to fight in defense of South Vietnam. A bold Communist strategy, exploiting the advantages given them by Geneva, can create a situation which may well lead to a new catastrophe for Vietnam and for the west.

I hesitate to approach this difficult subject. Let me begin with a personal assurance. If I express doubts created by information critical of your regime and if I ask you questions which seem to imply criticism on my part, I do it in a spirit of respect and friendship for your person and driven only by concern for the cause which you represent.

Let me begin by telling you that I find myself now the recipient of a great deal of counter-propaganda against your regime which is coming partly from Saigon and partly from Paris. Various groups, persons and of course a variety of motives are behind these attempts to influence me in a direction unfavorable to your policy. Most of what these people say can be completely disregarded but some of it I must take seriously partly because every policy is subject to a certain amount of criticism and partly because I am as yet in no position to judge the merit of every new point of view in Vietnamese politics. It would be presumptuous on my part to continue my activities without making an effort in a frank discussion with you to lift my judgment of the complicated affairs of your country above its present level.

To give you one example, I am now receiving material from Paris containing the complaints the Vietnamese Socialist party has against your government. I have received such material from Paris directly and also from the Socialist Bureau in London, which is a central office of the Socialist parties in the west. Through this Socialist Bureau all the Socialist parties in the west have been informed about the complaints of the Vietnamese Socialist party against your government. Some of these complaints have already found expression in the press of a number of Socialist parties in Eurpoes. As you know, I lived in Paris for a long time before the war where I became acquainted with many of the leading French Socialists. I am therefore not surprised that they would try to appeal to me at the urging of their Vietnamese friends. Frankly, I have no idea who these Vietnamese Socialist are. Also, the material I received from these sources does not impress me very favorably. I could reply to these people without your assistance but they are not the only ones and the fact that they have already found contacts here and caused some uneasiness among some Americans made me wonder whether it was right for me to ignore these criticisms instead of trying to discuss them with you or someone in your confidence who has the time and the knowledge to give me the information I need.

During the last few weeks I have heard more criticisms through an acquaintance I made in the course of my work in defending your government. I have met Mr. Milton Sacks, an old champion, in spite of his youth, of the cause of a free Vietnam and a man whom you can justly count among your strongest supporters and admirers in the United States. Mr. Sacks told me that he had known you already in the United States and saw you last in Paris at the end of 1953. He also told me that he had at that time already urged you to engage a public relations firm in order to organize information and propaganda for your government in this country. Mr. Sacks, as you probably know, has been severely—and I think unjustly—criticized by American officials for his anti-French position during the time when unconditional support of the French in Indochina was still United States policy. He has been working for many years on a book about Vietnam. I venture to say that Mr. Sacks is probably one of the best informed men on the subject of Vietnam in the United States. I was glad to meet him and he was very happy when he first heard of my efforts and of the relatively good effect which these efforts had on public opinion and in Washington. Mr. Sacks asked me to convey to you his warmest greetings, his compliments and his best wishes for your success. But he also asked me to take up the matter of your political strategy and to ask you a few questions which have been bothering him as well as myself.

Among the many contacts which Mr. Sacks has with Vietnamese friends, he has also one to a Socialist leader whose name I learned since I have met Mr. Sacks. I am sure you know all these people and are probably also acquainted with Mr. Ho Huu Tuong. I know nothing about him personally. Mr. Sacks is inclined to think well of him. Although I dislike pronouncing a political judgment on the basis of a person's writings, I would like to say that I was agreeably surprised by the quality of a document I read from the pen of Mr. Tuong. In all basic respects, as for instance in regard to the Vietminh, the French, the sects and the need for United States support for your policy, there is hardly a difference between your stand and his and little between your arguments and his. In spite of his ideological bias Mr. Tuong seems to be well aware of the immediate practical problems of Vietnamese policy in the present circumstances. Of course I do not know what he is doing and in what manner he is trying to make his views known and to implement his policy. I also do not know whether he has any following at all, and if he has one whether he is in control of his following. Not knowing the person and knowing only his writing which may be in contradiction to his actions, I cannot appraise the validity of his criticism. Nevertheless, the fact that he cannot freely express his opinions in South Vietnam, that he at least feels that his activity must remain underground, and he himself remain in hiding for fear of being persecuted, must be disturbing to most Americans. On the basis of the one document I read I cannot see why Mr. Tuong should not be free to work for his opinions among the nationalists in South Vietnam, the more so as he affirms his willingness to cooperate with all other groups and particularly also under your leadership.

I mention Mr. Tuong, although he is not the only one of whom I know either directly or through Mr. Sacks. Most of these people I am sure represent dissident small groups with very little influence. But your country is not as yet blessed with an abundance of popular leaders. The lack of a democratic period in your development is sufficient explanation for this fact. Under these circumstances it seems to me that every one sincerely devoted to the nationalist cause, no matter what temporary difficulties his temperament may cause, and even if his criticism would remain largely negative, should be allowed to take part in the anti-Communist struggle.

Let me add at this point that Mr. Sacks, in spite of the many complaints and accusations he receives, has always defended your government, and in particular defended your efforts to unify the country against the opposition of certain elements in the sects. In a long discussion with him we both agreed that this policy must find American support also in the future.

In raising these questions I am completely aware of the fact that I cannot judge the merit of any of these accusations and complaints. As I said before I have been disregarding them completely up to now, and I am willing to continue to disregard them if somebody can show to me convincingly that concessions to these groups would mean opening the door to other elements intent upon destroying whatever you have already achieved. But the question is not what I am willing to accept on the basis of my political understanding which, as you realize, is not universal and which I myself am only gradually acquiring through study and information. The question is rather how we are going to counteract the influence which these groups will acquire. Everyone who opposes your stand on the Geneva Treaty, in particular the French, but also the British, will, in the coming international discussion, use the complaints of these people as a main point against the validity of your claims as to the nature of your regime. This will seriously threaten our chances to convert the American people and its leaders to a more positive stand in favor of defending South Vietnam. Believe me that we are facing a serious problem which I personally shall be unable to handle unless my present information from yourself and your immediate surroundings is increased and extended to the problems which I am bringing to your attention today.

To emphasize my dilemma I must discuss the problem under a different personal aspect.

Several weeks before my departure from Saigon I was approached by a group of people whom I had not met before and of whose existence I had not known. They introduced themselves as the spokesmen of a political movement known under the name of Dai Viet. Eager to learn as much as I could about the complex political situation of your country I listened to them carefully and actually saw them a second time several days before leaving Saigon. At that time I was rather surprised to be approached by these people. I had not taken any political position in public and not done anything to give them the idea that I possessed political influence either in Saigon or in the United States. It is true that I had not made a secret of the opinions that I had acquired after the first several weeks in Vietnam, which are those I have expressed in talking and in writing ever since I returned to the United States. But neither I nor anyone else could have known at the time that I was going to play any part at all in the development of American opinion and American attitudes toward South Vietnam.

Having been engaged in conspiratorial policies myself, I was acquainted with the motivations of underground or semi-legal politicians who are always on the look-out for someone willing to listen to them and who may as often approach the right people as the wrong. I cannot deny that they had some political foresight when they approached me and spent much time and effort in an attempt to convince me that your policy was wrong.

I do not think it is necessary for me to give you a detailed description of everything they told me about Vietnam, about your government and your role in this phase of the struggle for national independence. It will certainly be no news to you to hear that they were extremely critical of your policies and on the whole unfriendly to your person. I have myself been the subject of most fierce personal attacks during the period of my own political activities and was therefore not very disturbed by the bitterness of tone or by the extreme nature of the arguments employed against you. The fact is that I instantly felt that these people were less your enemies than very disappointed friends: their bitterness came from a feeling of being rejected by you rather than a desire to impose themselves and their views on you.

Before I left Saigon these people told me that their leader, Dr. Nguyen Ton Hoan, was on a trip abroad and would probably be in Washington by the time I came home. They begged me to see Dr. Hoan and talk to him. I met Dr. Hoan briefly during my first visit to Washington after my return but became acquainted with him only after I returned from my vacation in Europe at the end of March. I saw Dr. Hoan several times before he left the United States about two months ago, and I met him again last week when he returned from France. I hasten to tell you that I have taken great pleasure in getting acquainted with Dr. Hoan. I was agreeably surprised by the maturity of his judgments as well as by the measured tone in which his criticism was presented. Our discussions were as frank as they were friendly and I admit that I have learned a great deal through this encounter. There never was a moment of embarrassment in our discussions which usually centered around your person, your political methods and the chances of survival for a free Vietnam under your leadership. Whether Dr. Hoan's sensible attitude in his talks with me is due to this temperament and his convictions or whether there was a great deal of tactical caution involved, the fact remains that his criticism of your policies was always on a highly objective level and that every reservation concerning your person was made in a tone of great respect. This alone made me like him and made me regret the fact that his talents and his energy are at present not at your service.

With respect to Dr. Hoan there is only one thing that bothers me a little and that is the fact that I have not talked to you about this encounter sooner. The reason is in part lack of time—everything else I did seemed so much more urgent—but in part it was also a desire to be sure myself about the nature of the conflict between your government and the movement represented by Dr. Hoan.

Unfortunately, I have not come to any satisfactory conclusion and if I am turning to you today it is not in order to give advice or to offer mediation, but rather to beg you to tell me your side of the story.

At the risk of simplifying the matter I will state how I see Dr. Hoan's position. There seems to be no difference in your and his aims. If he made reservations as to your methods in dealing with the sects, he was nevertheless ready to admit that the matter had to be settled one way or another. He is bitter about your alleged refusal to let other genuine nationalist forces cooperate in the work of your government but his bitterness does not lead him to a refusal to work under your leadership. As a matter of fact what hurt him most in recent times was your apparent unwillingness to discuss matters again with him or with other nationalist elements in a similar position. He had hoped that your brother Mr. Nhu would contact him while in Paris and renew a discussion which was broken off last year. I say this not in order to criticize your or your brother's attitude but rather to inform you of a fact of which you might not be wholly aware. I think that Dr. Hoan's position toward the chief of state, toward the question of unifying the country by settling the problem of the sects, toward the methods best suited to fight the Communists, and toward the problem of your relations with France or the United States, is basically identical with your own.

If Dr. Hoan saw me repeatedly and desires to see me again it is certainly not because he nourishes any hope to win me over to his side and to make me an ally of his against you. I think he is honest when he tells me that he does not want to fight against you. He wants to fight for his country.

As to my own position I think I have made it clear enough in my writings. Whenever I discuss matters with people critical of your policy, and I am not speaking only of Dr. Hoan, I am unequivocal in your defense. In spite of everything I have said in this letter I am as sure today as I was six months ago that your policies up to now were not inspired by any undemocratic sentiment or guided toward any undemocratic aims. I know the circumstances which required the measure taken by you. I know the counterforces which had to be fought and could be fought only in a certain way, and I know also the dangers which a different policy would have created. But your very success has created a situation which may possibly require new methods if further progress is to be achieved. Freedoms which some people might have abused with deadly results for your regime have perhaps ceased to be a danger even if the people who use and misuse them have not basically changed. *There is a point in the development toward democratic institutions in which the compromising with democratic freedoms becomes ten times more dangerous than the harm that individuals can do in using or misusing these freedoms.*

Again, it is far from my mind to give you advice. All I would like to express is how the problem looks to someone who has to defend you against this kind of criticism in the United States where, as you know, every infringement on freedom is frowned upon as a serious disease of the political body. You must know that I have nothing to gain or to lose no matter what methods you adopt in laying the foundations for a democratic Vietnam. I have great sympathy for people like Dr. Hoan and although I may be entirely mistaken I believe, or rather I feel, that he has qualities not only as a human being but also as a man of politics. And even if you should feel that nothing could be gained for your regime by cooperating with Dr. Hoan, I still feel that once the power to harm your regime is taken away from your organized opponents in the sects and once French policy is reduced to the expression of dissatisfaction with your cause, *all criticisms by other nationalists should be allowed free expression.* Up to now nobody has given to the Vietnamese people what a politically alert nation must have: the right to complain about its government, to make proposals, to criticize its leaders, to discuss and, of course, also to unjustly abuse the government. The more this need can find expression, the less harmful it will become.

It is in this connection that the question of an assembly which you are planning to have elected becomes extremely important from the point of view also of American support for your regime. Many of the present antagonisms in the nationalist camp could be wiped out if such an assembly were to be elected soon. Every existing political group that is not bought by foreign interests or connected with the Communists should be given freedom to seek representation in such an assembly. A generous political amnesty would probably help to create a climate of nationalist solidarity in which such an election campaign would develop in a spirit positive to your leadership. Once the assembly is in existence discontent can be voiced legally and in the formal frame of a democratic institution which by its mere functioning reduces the excesses of all extremists. The more the various leaders can speak and put themselves forward, the less they will feel inclined to conspire, to go underground, or to ally themselves with politically doubtful elements. There is no real politician who would not rather talk from a visible stage than to conspire with people whom he does not really consider his friends and with whom he may get tied up only out of despair.

Now you may think that I have gone too far in defending your critics. Please tell me so if this is your feeling. I beg you to accept my frankness as a sign of respect and as an expression of deep concern even if you have to reject the criticism which is implied in my questions and doubts. In conclusion I would like to assure you of one thing: no matter what your reaction is to my letter, I shall continue my efforts to mobilize American support for your policy to secure freedom in peace for the people of Vietnam.

Sincerely,

Here is my translation of Diem's reply:

Saigon, 29 May 1956

Dear Mr. Buttinger:

In the course of recent repairs done in my office, my staff discovered, slipped in between two drawers, my answer to your letter of August 1955 . . . Please excuse this involuntary delay which has left you for such a long time in a state of unrelieved anxiety for Vietnam, for which you have so much active friendship.

But this inconvenience has its happy side for me. Because it gave me a reason for reading once again—with profound emotion—this old letter of yours, full of sympathy for my country, and charged with scruples (concerns) which do the writer credit.

Your letter is remarkable as well for its clarity. For you predicted a year ahead what would be the Communist maneuvers around the concept of "general elections," a term to which the free world is so sensitive, as a device for absorbing South Vietnam. You have been able to recognize the extent to which we followed your advice by organizing free elections in the South, despite all the attempts of the Viet Cong to sabotage them, and despite the interested misgivings of the parties that call themselves nationalist.

A number of other questions you raised in this letter have been resolved in ways that imposed themselves. Despite the fact that time has answered many of the things that preoccupied you at that time, I would nonetheless like to pick up our conversation again on this subject, because I believe it is difficult for you to go to the heart of men and things in this country as I have. However, I would not wish this experience on you.

A colonial domination of nearly 100 years and ten years of an atrocious war, have not been without their profound effects on Vietnam, in her body and above all in her soul. The generation of men who could constitute the ruling elite of the country have all been formed in French schools, where it was fashionable, at the time they were there, to affect an elegant skepticism towards all serious things, an attitude of detachment and secularism.

France paid and is still paying dearly for the moral and intellectual slackness of the period from 1930 to 1940. As a reaction from this decadent culture, other young Vietnamese have thrown themselves into Fascism or Communism. It is from among this latter group that the Communist parties in Indochina were born, as follows in chronological order—Quoc-dan-Dang, Cao-Dai, Dai-Viet, Hoa Hao. Contrary to the Communists, who received a good education (formation serieuse), the Vietnamese nationalist *and Fascist* parties, deserted by the intellectuals whose ideal is not to become involved, have therefore not played parts of any importance either for the Viet Minh or for anyone else, our nationalist parties are very mediocre from the point of view of doctrine as well as organization.

That is why they were so easily eliminated by the Viet Minh and domesticated by the colonialists. Unrealistic and immoral, they think it is sufficient to call themselves anti-communist to beat down communism, and they believe all they have to do is call themselves revolutionaries in order for everything under the sun to be permitted them. In the programs of all these parties you won't find a word against feudalism or against the Sects System.

Besides, despite their declarations, not one of these parties ever seriously believed that communism could be resisted. I only realized this six months after I took power. When I was at Orly getting ready to take the plane to return to my country as President of the Council in Saigon, Mr. Hoang Xuan Han told me that he would place himself at my disposal only if I were willing to negotiate with the Viet Minh. Mr. Nguyen Manh Ha on the other hand was making a last grab for the realization of his coexistence plan. Mr. Ho Huu Tuong, ex-Trotskyite and even more dishonest than the others, was concealing from you his "Trung Lap Che" program, meaning precisely *neutralism*, which was intended as a screen for co-existence under the instructions of the Viet Minh. By the intermediacy of his brother, a Communist agent, Ho Huu Tuong was in communication with Pham Cong Tac to bring the Cao-Dai into the Viet Minh's game. The chief political and confidential agent of Pham Cong Tac, a Cao-Dai Lieutenant Colonel, revealed that all these intrigues began since July 1954, after a meeting between Tac and Pham Van Dong at Geneva.

This is why Ho Huu Tuong proposed to "furnish him the indispensable financial means for setting up a neutralist movement in the Plaine des Jones, which will have been previously declared autonomous." This is the same Ho Huu Tuong who was pushing Bay-Vien, whose political adviser he became, into breaking out war against the Government. At the time he was complaining to you about being hunted by the Government, Ho Huu Tuong was traveling freely between Paris and Saigon. Besides, everyone knows that he had no means of his own to make trips of that sort with such frequency. As for Mr. Nguyen Ton Hoan, he refused *three times* to work with me, on the grounds that the portfolio of Minister of National Defense and nothing less was alone worthy of his ambitions. Besides, neither the Cao Dai, nor the Bing Xuyen, nor the Hoa Hao would have gone along with this man getting that post, since all the Sects were conspiring to get it for themselves. It is true that Nguyen Ton Hoan did tell me that he could fill this position "in cooperation with the little Hoa Hao chief Lam Thanh Nguyen, and that if he couldn't have that job he would settle for Ambassador in Bangkok." As a matter of fact, the real dream of Nguyen Ton Hoan has always been to become chief of a new Sect, the Dai Viet, with an army and a zone of his own. He has always pursued this dream with relentless eagerness. He collaborated with the French to have a zone of his own. Unfortunately, the chief of the Dai Viet commando which the French located in Cai Lay, which could become the nucleus of a new Sect, disaffiliated from Nguyen Ton Hoan to work for his own account. At this point Nguyen Ton Hoan went back to this friend Lam Thanh Nguyen, the little Cao-Dai Chief of Chan-Doc, who was trying to get from me the province of Ha Tien, on the Gulf of Siam, as the price of his fidelity, which deal was being promoted most enthusiastically by Nguyen Ton Hoan. When Nguyen Ton Hoan had said he would settle for the post of Ambassador at Bangkok, one of his reasons was to give a hand to Lam Thanh Nguyen (arms traffic, building a maquis in Thailand out of Vietnamese refugees with the assistance of his friend's, Hoa Hao men) and another was that he didn't believe an effective nationalist resistance possible either against the Viet Minh or the French. This is exactly what he told my brother Ngo Dinh Nhu when he asked the latter to intervene on his behalf with the Binh Xuyen, then in control of the Surete and the issuance of visas—so he could get to France.

When Nguyen Ton Hoan refused to be a part of the central government, I ordered an offer to be extended to the Dai Viet to collaborate on other echelons. This is how they came to be given the Sureté, the Police, and the provincial militia of the important province of Quang Tri on the 17th Parallel. But Nguyen Ton Hoan, who led them to believe they would get support from the Americans and the French, ordered his partisans in Quang Tri, Thua Thien, in collusion with Nguyen Van Hinh's partisans, and with the encouragement of the French, to become dissidents and formed an underground at Ba Long. Though armed and supplied by the French, they were however crushed almost immediately, because most of the troops who had followed them abandoned them as soon as they realized they had been betrayed by them. Nguyen Ton Hoan's Dai Viets are actually at the present taking asylum with the French, first in Camp Chanson where the French built them a powerful transmitter with which they pelted our government everyday with manure-laden propaganda, and afterward at Seno, where they are continuing their task of traitors. Recently Vietnam Presse published a letter from Nguyen Ton Hoan to Guy Mollet asking France to intervene for the protection of Vietnam. Nguyen Ton Hoan is not the only example of a politician, without serious training, seeking to win power by force, which he hasn't got at his disposal anyway. Others try to work on a group of dissident Cao Daists to carry out the dream of a fascist coup d'etat with help from outside, such as this Phan Quang Dan who deceived the Cao Dai General Nguyen Thanh Phuong by making him believe he had the support of the American Democratic Party, whose favorite Phan Quang Dan is supposed to be. Already one of their group, Nguyen Bao Toan, has set up shop in New York where he went after stealing five million piasters, the entire funds of the Dan Xa party of the Hoa Hao led by General Nguyen Giac Ngo, who is waiting for him here to make him cough it up.

SAIGON, le 29 Mai , 1955

PERSONNELLE

Cher Monsieur BUTTINGER,

C'est au cours des récentes réparations dans
mon bureau que mes services ont découvert, glissée
entre deux tiroirs, ma réponse a votre lettre d'Août
1955 ...Je vous prie de vouloir bien excuser ce retard
involontaire qui vous a laissé si longtemps avec vos
inquiétudes au sujet du Vietnam pour lequel vous avez
tant d'amitié agissante.

C'est un contretemps qui comporte cependant
un côté heureux, pour moi. Car il m'a donné l'occasion
de relire - avec une profonde émotion - votre vieille
lettre, toute pleine de symphathie pour mon pays et
aussi toute imprégnée de scrupules qui font honneur
a son auteur.

Elle est aussi remarquable par la lucidité.
Car, un an a l'avance, vous avez prévu les manoeuvres
communistes qui, sous le mot "élections générales"
auquel le monde libre est sensible, cherchent en réa-
lité a absorber le Vietnam Sud. Vous avez pu vous
rendre compte que nous avons suivi vos conseils en
organisant des élections libres dans la zône Sud,
malgré toutes les tentatives de sabotage des Viet Cong
et malgré aussi les craintes intéressées des partis
dits nationalistes.

Nombre d'autres questions soulevées par vous
dans cette lettre ont reçu des solutions qui s'impo-
saient. Malgré que le temps ait répondu a pas mal de
vos préoccupations d'alors, je tiens cependant a
reprendre avec vous la conversation sur ce sujet, car
je pense qu'il est difficile pour vous d'aller au fonds
des choses et des hommes de ce pays comme je l'ai fait.
Ce que d'ailleurs je ne vous souhaite pas ...

Une domination ....

Facsimile of the first and last pages of Diem's letter, in French.

Si nous pensons que les autres pays du Sud Est Asiatique qui n'ont pas les mêmes difficultés que nous, ont mis, les uns, cinq ans, les autres huit ans pour avoir une Constitution, nous devons estimer que nous avons quelque mérite a devenir , en si peu de temps, ce que nous sommes. La situation est certainement meilleure qu'il y a un an . Mais nous sommes dans l'année de la décision, où il ne peut y avoir de place pour les aventuriers et les amateurs. Face a un ennemi implacable, et maîte dans l'art politique, nous devons opposer un front solide, sans fissure a tous les points de vue.

C'est vous dire, cher Monsieur BUTTINGER, combien j'apprécie l'effort que vous et nos amis êtes en train de faire la-bas pour nous soutenir. J'espère que vous trouverez une occasion pour revenir ici, au Vietnam ou vous êtes certain de trouver l'accueil le plus chaleureux. Par la même occasion, vous pourrez emmener M. SACHS avec vous, car il n'est pas facile d'écrire l'histoire actuelle du peuple vietnamien de Paris. Depuis deux ans, il y a eu de grands changements ici. Sur place, vous verrez mieux de quoi cela retourne.

Mais je m'aperçois que l'heure avance et qu'il faut que je me rende aux audiences. En attendant le plaisir de vous revoir bientot, veuillez croire, cher Monsieur BUTTINGER, a mes sentiments les meilleurs.

Ngo Dinh Diem

This Nguyen Bao Toan, who now talks the language of a pure democrat, is the man who always opposed elections in the Southern zone. How many times did he come running to me insisting that I not have recourse to elections to realize the National Assembly, on pretext that the Viet Minh would surely win out and that it was wiser to seek approval by referendum of a presidium composed of members of the different parties whom I was probably meant to designate. Actually, none of these gentlemen dared show himself as a candidate in the elections of last March, for since they had no credit with the people they were afraid of being beaten.

Here are some of the types who pretend to be able to govern this country, in the midst of the exceptional circumstances through which Viet Nam is currently passing. Even the most liberal ruling powers always make provision for a transitional system for a people passing from the status of a colony to the situation of an independent nation, for fear there might be a retrogression into servitude under the internal feudal elements still in being, or because of a shortage of competent people to run the government, or to protect the country from the ambitions of another foreign imperialism. When we look at the difficulties that beset us every day from every quarter, we Vietnamese, who have had to press on without pause while the organism of our state was eaten away by a great Communist cancer, we are almost at the point of believing these aforementioned powers may be quite right in their thinking. But it would be treason to our destiny to abandon ourselves to the temptation of easy solutions which are no more than illusions anyway. Because nothing is easy in the life of a man, or a people. The essential thing is to have an ideal and try to realize it despite all wind and weather. Is this not the very essence of democracy?

For democracy is not something achieved once and for all, but rather "a perservering effort of quest for the proper means of assuring mankind of the maximum of liberty, the maximum of responsibility, and the greatest opportunity for the life of the spirit." (See my message to the National Assembly, April 17, 1956) Our purpose is to create with the means at hand and within the limits history imposes upon us, an *open regime*, as distinguished from a closed system built around one man or one party.

In the course of our struggle and our progress, our path is getting wider everyday, with God's help. Already we have an elected Assembly. Tomorrow we will have a Constitution. When we think of how the other countries of Southeast Asia, who didn't have the difficulties we did have, needed some of them five years, some of them eight, just to get a Constitution, we can justly feel that there must be some merit in our having become what we are now in so short a time. The situation is certainly better than it was last year. But we are now in the year of decision, where there is no room for adventurers and amateurs. Face to face with an impossible enemy, a master in the art of politics, we must present a solid front of opposition, with no fissure showing from any angle.

This is to tell you, my dear Mr. Buttinger, how much I appreciate the effort which you and our friends are making over there to sustain us. I hope you will find an opportunity to return here, to Viet Nam, where you can be assured of the warmest kind of welcome. On this occasion you can take Mr. Sacks along with you, because it is not easy to write the contemporary history of the Vietnamese people from Paris. Within the last two years there have been great changes here. You will be able to see what is going on much better on the spot.

But I see that it's late and I must get ready for my appointment. Meanwhile, looking forward to the pleasure of seeing you again soon, please believe, my dear Mr. Buttinger, that I send you my very best wishes.

NGO DINH DIEM

The Diem dictatorship forced a great number of non-Communist South Vietnamese into exile. In the summer of 1961 several of these democrats contacted me both in Paris and in New York and made proposals for an appeal to the Vietnamese people, on the basis of which I wrote the following document, printed in Paris, which they signed and then had clandestinely distributed, in French and Vietnamese, throughout part of South Vietnam.

TO THE ENSLAVED AND OPPRESSED PEOPLE OF VIETNAM! TO THE MEN AND WOMEN OF THE WORLD WHO LIVE IN FREEDOM!

Seven years after the Geneva Agreement, which brought the Indochina war to an end but divided our country into two mutilated halves, the Vietnamese people have achieved neither true independence nor the freedom for which they have waged its long and heroic struggle. Today, our people are not only victimized by two dictatorships which, in spite of their conflicting aims, are equally determined to rule by force; the people of Vietnam are now again suffering the cruelties of a murderous and devastating war.

The South, to which seven years ago most Vietnamese attached their desperate hopes for freedom and social justice, has developed, under the one-man rule of Ngo Dinh Diem, into a political wasteland from which freedom has been driven out by fraud and force.

In the Free World, to which Ngo Dinh Diem continues to appeal for help, his regime, although deeply discredited, can still mobilize sympathy and support through impudent political deception. At home, where his deception no longer works, his regime rests entirely on privileges for a small group of docile followers and on the use of force against all others. To obtain support from abroad, Diem praises the ideals of the Free World. But his muzzled press, his rigged elections, his rubber stamp National Assembly and his concentration camps for democratic opponents make a mockery of democracy and human rights.

Diem's methods of rule have contributed nothing to the defense of the South. On the contrary. Because the Vietnamese have long been tired of Diem's claim that the country can remain free only if the people are deprived of freedom, and because Diem himself lacks all the qualities of a popular leader and great organizer, his rule by force, far from producing national unity and military strength, is undermining both. Upright men and women who placed service to the people above subservience to the ruling clique have been systematically eliminated and subsequently slandered. The administration has thus been turned into a bureaucratic machine whose masters have killed initiative, promoted inefficiency, allowed conspicuous waste and opened the door to corruption.

What is true for the civil administration is unfortunately true also for the army. Initiative is regarded as insubordination, promotion in the higher ranks is contingent on total submission to the President's judgment and will rather than on achievement in organization or combat. First-rate officers who are slow in public praise of Diem or too popular with their units never get a chance to play an important role in the ongoing military struggle. Moreover, the personal character of the regime deprives the fight conducted by the army of its true national significance, while the hatred of the people for the regime prevents the army from obtaining the popular support that is indispensable for effective anti-guerilla action.

Because the short-lived hopes for a free and strong South have been destroyed by the Diem regime, the Vietnamese people as a whole are now forced to go through another bloody and tragic phase in their long struggle for independence and freedom. Once again the country is experiencing the miseries of a war whose aims are not those of the vast majority of our people, either of the North or the South. The people of the North, although silenced by their oppressors, oppose the transformation of the entire country into a province of the communist block as firmly as the people of the South. But even if a chance should open up for them to rise, at the risk of their lives, against their ruthless masters, they would never rise, nor could we expect them to rise, as long as the South fails to give them the inspiring example of a regime dedicated to freedom, justice, and welfare.

Aware of our responsibility at this crucial hour in the history of Vietnam, the undersigned, Vietnamese patriots devoted to the realization of independence for our country and freedom for our people, appeal to the men and women of the world who cherish freedom, to the statesmen who still support the Diem regime, and to the governments who condemn Communist aggression if directed against their own country:

Lend your moral support to the citizens of Vietnam, at home and abroad, who are trying to replace the crumbling regime of Ngo Dinh Diem in order to create a truly free and prosperous South—a country and a political system worth the sacrifices required for its defense.

The creation at Saigon, as quickly as possible, of a free and strong regime of national unity is now the main condition for the defeat of the present Communist attempt to conquer the South by force. But more than that; it is also the only hope we have for the eventual realization of our ultimate aim: the reunification of Vietnam under the banner of total national independence, with the fullest institutional safeguards for political and religious freedom, and for the exercise, defense, and further development of democracy as our way of life.

To our compatriots in the South, irrespective of religion, class and racial origin, we appeal to rally behind the men and women who have rejected the Diem regime—not because it opposes Communism, but rather because it has become, in its methods and its treatment of the human being, too much like the tyranny of which it falsely claims to be a total negation.

In our struggle for a free and strong South, for which the undersigned will prepare the outline of a program for discussion and dissemination, we can count on much sympathy in every part of the world. But neither the overthrow of Diem nor the defeat of Communist aggression can result from actions undertaken by foreign supporters of a free Vietnam. These tasks must be accomplished by the Vietnamese themselves, above all by the people of the South.

PART Two

The Second Indochina War

*L*ike the First Indochina war, the Second Indochina war too was said to have been started by the Communists. Since not only the Administration and our military leaders, but also Congress and the press expounded this claim during a decade of American military intervention in Indochina, it is important to re-examine the question.

I.
Who Started the War?

There is no lack of statements by American political leaders blaming the Second Indochina war on Communist aggression, usually combined with an assurance that aggression will fail. Ambassador Henry Cabot Lodge, for instance, said in an interview in Saigon on September 28, 1964: "Once the Vietcong and Hanoi have been convinced that this attempt at aggression is doomed to failure, they will stop." And President Johnson, while already contemplating the bombing of North Vietnam and the sending of American combat forces to the South, stated in a speech in Bergen, New Jersey on October 14, 1964: "With our help, the people of South Vietnam can defeat Communist aggression."

Aggression was not only Communist but also "external," as both Secretary of State Dean Rusk and Assistant Secretary George W. Ball assured the American people. On February 25, 1965, after the beginning of systematic American bombing of North Vietnam, Rusk stated: "I think pacification of [South Vietnam] would be easy if external aggression were stopped." And Ball in several speeches at this time called the war in Vietnam a cynical and systematic aggression by the North Vietnamese.

To support this view, Rusk repeatedly stated—denying overwhelming evidence to the contrary—that the Vietcong and its political arm, the National Liberation Front, had no popular support, or, as Ball put it: "The war in Vietnam has few attributes of an indigenous revolt." On June 23, 1965 Rusk claimed that there was "no evidence that the Vietcong has any significant popular following in South Vietnam"—a statement he repeated verbally on May 10 and reconfirmed on May 30, 1965 when, for the TV audience watching the program *Meet the Press*, he said: "We do not believe that this National Liberation Front has any strong base among the South Vietnamese people."

Nobody, however, sank as low as General Maxwell D. Taylor, supposedly one of our most intelligent military leaders, who claimed on the CBS program *Face the Nation* on February 13, 1966, that the guerrillas in South Vietnam were pure ethnic North Vietnamese, and that this proved the foreign character of the war. Anyone who has learned from the Pentagon Papers that the U. S. airforce and army were sent to Vietnam because the guerrillas threatened to overthrow the Saigon regime before a single North Vietnamese soldier was fighting in the South (something Taylor must have known), will have no trouble recognizing his statement as a lie. Besides, even if the guerrillas had really been ethnic North Vietnamese, they would still not have been foreigners in the South, for they are just as genuinely Vietnamese as any southener.

The truth about aggression in Vietnam is plain enough. It was not the Communists who started the war. Why should they, being sure of total victory through the 1956 elections? The war began when President Diem, in the summer of 1955 and again during 1956 sent his army into regions of the South which the Vietminh, due to popular support, still effectively controlled. It was in response to this form of aggression and after having been denied certain victory through the peaceful means of elections that the Communists too gradually began to use force. Their armed reaction, however, became an organized insurrection only three years after Diem's resort to force, and far from being "external" this revolt must be recognized as having been for many years exclusively indigenous.

This does not mean that Hanoi did not favor and support the revolt in the South. It did; but it did not express that support by sending parts of its army. Until March, 1965, nearly all the infiltrators from the North—4,500 by the end of 1964— were Southerners who had gone North after the Geneva cease-fire of 1954. But the struggle in the South would have remained, at least until 1965, a civil war within one nation even if more than a small number of political and military advisers from Hanoi had taken part in it— unless one has been converted to the absurd notion that any Vietnamese born above the 17th parallel is a foreigner in Vietnam. "To us," a Vietnamese friend once told me, "this sounds as it would sound to you if the people in Florida or Texas claimed that anyone born in New England is not an American but a foreigner." (Very few Americans knew that three of the eleven Hanoi politburo members were southerners.)

For those who refer to the presence of foreigners in South Vietnam to prove that the war was the result of external aggression, the logical conclusion should be that the aggressor of the Second Indochina war was the United States.

Indeed, Diem's army was trained by Americans, armed and paid for by the United States. And two years before the first battalion of regular North Vietnamese troops crossed the 17th parallel— between 400 and 500 men according to Secretary of Defense McNamara—the number of so-called American military advisors in the ranks of the South Vietnamese army stood at 16,500.

Although President Johnson, after having started to bomb the North in February and to send the first group of U. S. Marines into the South in March, 1965, stated at least half a dozen times that "we

seek no wider war" (on March 25, April 1, and April 25, for instance), the number of American combat troops stood at 148,000 by
the end of October 1965.

After learning this, I was shocked whenever I met an intelligent
American who still believed a word of the man who in several
speeches before the presidential elections of 1964 had firmly announced he would not send American soldiers to Vietnam. On August 12, 1964, Johnson, in a speech in New York City, criticized
those who "call upon us to supply American boys to do the job that
Asian boys should do." On September 25, 1964, he added to a
similar statement that "we don't want to get tied down in a land war
in Asia." Three years later, toward the end of 1967, the man who
had made these promises ordered more than half a million soldiers to
fight in Vietnam, ten times the number of North Vietnamese soldiers that had by then joined the Vietcong guerillas in the South.

These facts should make it impossible for any honest American
to deny Norman Mailer's conclusion after the end of the Second
Indochina war that "the responsibility for the war is entirely ours."

II.
Defense of Freedom?

Between the Tonking resolution of Congress in August, 1964 and a
remark by President Ford almost eleven years later, one could easily
collect a hundred official American statements asserting that defense
of freedom was the goal pursued by the United States in Vietnam.
The way Congress put it was that "the United States is assisting the
peoples of Southeast Asia to protect their freedom," while President
Ford, at a press conference on June 9, 1975, said that one of the
lessons of Vietnam was "that we have to work with other governments that feel as we do that freedom is vitally important."

I do not think it necessary any longer to prove to the American
reader that the absence of real freedom was a feature common to all
Saigon regimes from Diem's police state to Thieu's brutal and politically ineffective dictatorship. Since when is freedom "vitally important" to a government which has suspended all civil rights, abolished

freedom of the press and assembly, made illegal every political party except its own, and put into prison anyone who dared to criticize its policy? And since when is a country free if its government is headed by a man (Vice Air Marshal Ky) whose hero was Hitler; and later by a president elected as a one-man candidate with the kind of majority so far obtained only under fascist or Communist totalitarian regimes?

There are of course those for whom any dictatorship declaring itself anti-Communist, no matter how brutal, is by definition "free." But to make this a guiding principle of foreign policy, as America's political leaders did in Vietnam, results not merely from political self-deception. We are here dealing with much *conscious* deceit also, requiring a certain amount of political lying—one of the reasons why this kind of mindless anti-Communism has proved in Vietnam, and will prove everywhere else, politically ineffective.

I do not mean to say that everyone who still argues along these lines intends to deceive. There are always some whose perception of reality is so profoundly distorted by ideological obsessions that they actually believe their own nonsense. In politics this happens even to highly intelligent people. Proof is an article by William Buckley, who, in discussing Vietnam in *The New York Post* of April 22, 1975, reproached Anthony Lewis of *The New York Times* for wanting "that all conquered people should stay conquered, or that all free people quickly collapse in the face of aggression . . ." I cannot think of anything more disparaging to say than that Buckley really believes the South Vietnamese people were free during the last twenty years.

I would say the same of the group of Americans, still members of the long obsolete Friends of Vietnam who, in a paid advertisement in the *New York Times* of April 21, 1975, asked for more military aid to the Thieu regime, in order to enable the South Vietnamese people to "defend their freedom." Perhaps some of these Americans will now learn that even the powerful United States cannot save freedom where it does not exist.

In view of the many recent revelations of anti-democratic activities of the CIA at home and abroad, what its former head, Admiral William F. Raborn said on a TV program in July 1966 agrees well with the lack of truthfulness that characterized America's governmental propaganda in regard to Vietnam: "I think that the Central Intelligence Agency is but a small part of the national effort to perpetuate truly democratic ideals and freedom around the world."

In his review of Philip Agee's book *Inside the Company: CIA Diary*, Harrison E. Salisbury wrote in the *Saturday Review* of August 9, 1975:

> The CIA did not really notice that thanks to its efforts America's 'friends' around the world more and more became the antithesis of democracy—the military dictatorships of the Middle East, the purchasable colonels of Latin America, the Francos, the Salazars, the Shahs, the Chiang-Kai-Sheks, the shabby rulers of South Korea and South Vietnam. Without noticing, the CIA became more and more distrustful of the essentials of democracy—free choice, free speech, the democratic process.

Admiral Raborn's remark about the CIA was surpassed only by that of Senator Barry Goldwater, who informed the American people through *Newsweek* of September 21, 1964, that its mission was "to see freedom sent around the world," adding that this was "God's charge to us."

III.
Civilization, Morality and Vietnam

What Cardinal Spellman said, on December 26, 1966, surprised only those who were not acquainted with his views: "This war in Vietnam, I believe, is a war for civilization . . . American troops are there for the defense, protection and salvation not only of our country, but I believe of civilization itself."

This war for civilization, Vice President Spiro Agnew said in April 1972, will be recorded by history as "perhaps the most moral act the United States ever performed." Agnew's own conspicuous lack of political morals makes it easy to dismiss such a statement as despicable. Such easy dismissal is not possible for the statement that "our cause [in Vietnam] is not immoral," which Dr. Herman Kahn, the prominent director of the Hudson Institute, made in August 1966. If specific knowledge and a minimum of humanitarian concern

are lacking, an intelligent man like Herman Kahn may well call the
burning of villages and the murderous fire against places suspected
of concealing Vietcong guerrillas legitimate acts of war. In their
book *The Air War in Indochina* Raphael Littauer and Norman Upp-
hoff wrote: "Our bombs have destroyed villages of no military
value. At Nuremberg that was a war crime." Incredible as it may
sound today, Kahn not only thought that this type of warfare was
compatible with "the Christian just-war doctrine"; he also added
what one day may be regarded as the most incredible pronounce-
ment about the Vietnam war: "But I don't believe this has killed
anybody who is not guilty."

No less shocking, because of the man's reputation as a distinguished political spokesman, is a statement of Adlai Stevenson on
the CBS program *Face the Nation* in June 1964. Calling American
support for the Saigon regime "a matter of principle," he specified
that the United States was acting on behalf of the "morality and
conscience of the world."

Much that has been written about the Vietnamese war was simply stupid, but worse than stupid was what David Lawrence wrote
in an editorial of *U. S. News and World Report* of February 21, 1966.
Defining philanthropy as "love for mankind," he elaborated: "What
the United States is doing in Vietnam is the most significant example of philanthropy . . . that we have witnessed in our times." (This
statement reminded me of one made by the French General Jean de
Lattre de Tassigny in July 1951: "Not since the Crusades has France
undertaken such disinterested action.")

I have no doubt that future generations will be unable to understand how anyone of a normal mind and a minimum of human
feelings could have called moral, decent, philanthropic and Christian what the military forces of the United States did in Vietnam.
Once the true facts of this horrible war become generally known,
most Americans will ask: What is Christian about the indiscriminate
killing of civilians, the bombing of hospitals, the destruction of help-
less villages? What is moral about refusing to take prisoners or, if
any are taken, having them killed by the South Vietnamese army
after watching them being tortured? What is decent about throwing

a captured enemy soldier out of a flying helicopter in order to frighten a second one into supplying information? And was it really philanthropy on the part of the United States to supply the estimated $400,000 needed to kill a single Vietcong?

Crimes like killing civilians were not only committed but also defended as unavoidable in war—apparently with a bad conscience, since there was also an official policy of denying or at least minimizing the number of civilians killed by counting all the dead as Vietcong. An Associated Press dispatch of October 24, 1967 read as follows: "After a battle, all dead other than allied troops are counted as enemies, even women and children."

A small example of indiscriminate killing of civilians and then calling them Vietcong was reported by *The Washington Evening Star* on March 4, 1965. The paper quoted a U. S. pilot, just back from a raid as saying: "I killed 40 Vietcong today. That's the number they told me were in the village; anyway, I leveled it."

The killing of civilians was already an accepted method of eliminating a few guerillas suspected of being in a village when U. S. military involvement still consisted only in paying, supplying and "advising" the South Vietnamese army. The anti-Diem author Thich Nhat Hanh wrote in his book *Lotus in a Sea of Fire:* "The war has consistently seen more civilians killed than Vietcong. Between 1961 and 1964, even modest estimates of the casualties indicate that more than half a million civilians had been killed." And he added: "Under these circumstances, is it a matter of surprise that more and more Vietnamese are drawn to the ranks of the National Liberation Front?"

Of this, some Americans in Vietnam were well aware. *The New York Times* of September 24, 1969 quoted the following revealing statement of an officer: "They say this village is 80 per cent VC-supporters. By the time we are finished, it will be 95 per cent."

The killing of civilians was confirmed also by General David M. Shoup, a former commander of the U. S. Marine Corps and one of the earliest prominent Americans to oppose the war. He said in Los Angeles on May 14, 1966: "You read, you're televised, you're radioed to, you're preached to, that it is necessary that we have our armed forces fight, get killed and maimed, and kill and maim other human beings, including women and children . . ."

Statements like this, apt to change the American people's mind about the Vietnam war, upset men like Barry Goldwater, who, in a speech in New York on January 23, 1967, urged his fellow-Americans "to forget about this civilian stuff." (A report of the Kennedy Sub-committee on Refugees put the number of civilians killed in South Vietnam as of August, 1971 at 335,000 and the number of wounded at 740,000. The monthly civilian toll, killed and wounded under Johnson was 95,000, and under Nixon between January, 1969 and August, 1971, 130,000.)

I was not able to find more than one American political leader who agreed with Goldwater about "this civilian stuff" and also had the courage to say so. This was Congressman Mendel Rivers, Democrat of South Carolina, who was quoted by *U. S. News and World Report* of January 9, 1967, as having said: "We ought not even to consider civilians." Rivers and Goldwater must not have been bothered when they learned, from a National Security Study early in 1969, that American airstrikes over North Vietnam had killed 52,000 civilians. One was led to such an assumption on learning what Senator Allan Ellender said in a TV interview on January 15, 1970: that the more than three hundred women, children and sick old men massacred by American soldiers at My Lai "got just what they deserved."

Justice was no doubt well served in the eyes of such people by having our soldiers do what the commander of the U. S. Marine Corps, General Wallace Green, Jr., had said about his men that landed at Danang on March 6, 1965: "The one job I want them to do is to find the Vietcong and kill them." Being constantly subject to this kind of exhortation and seeing that no matter how many Vietnamese they killed there always were new ones to take their place, it is not too surprising if a good American soldier, convinced that he was fighting to save civilization, reached the conclusion that "the only thing to do is to kill everybody in the country over five years old." (Quoted by Robert Sherrod in *Life* magazine of January 27, 1967.)

One wonders how many Americans realized that we were killing more civilians than Vietcongs when they read in *Newsweek* of October 18, 1965, that "the U. S. Air Force flew 26,858 sorties in Vietnam in a single week," or after reading in the *Christian Science Monitor* of April 5, 1967, that by late 1966, the U. S. army in South Vietnam fired more than one million artillery shells monthly. This of course meant not only destroying hundreds of villages but also killing countless civilians who had learned too late that their homes belonged to what the army had proclaimed to be a "free-firing zone."

Another American responsibility for the murder of non-combatants was the so-called Operation Phoenix. On that subject, which Washington would now like never to be mentioned again, *The New York Times* wrote on June 11, 1975: "The CIA's involvement in the Vietnam war resulted in the Operation Phoenix . . . It resulted in the death of more than 20,000 'suspected' members of the 'Vietcong infrastructure' and allegedly in the torture of others." The total number of victims, according to the Agency for International Development, was: killed 20,587, jailed 28,778 and re-educated 17,717. (AID does not add that "re-education" required in most cases a certain amount of torture.) The Indochina Resource Center in Washington, often better informed than our intelligence services, claimed that the number of civilians murdered because they were suspected or denounced by personal enemies as Vietcong or Communist sympathizers, was 40,994. (The architect of Operation Phoenix was William E. Colby, later head of the CIA.)

It would of course be naive to believe that, in a conflict which retained aspects of a civil war, only one side would resort to terror and commit atrocities. However, no one has yet been able to prove Vietcong atrocities amounting to more than a fraction of this sort of crimes committed by our side. Abundant evidence for this unwelcome truth can be found in countless articles and books by shocked Americans and other non-Communist reporters. One of these, the Pulitzer Prize Winner Malcolm Browne, wrote that many a news correspondent or U. S. military advisor has seen Vietcong prisoners whose hands were whacked off with machetes by their captors.

When Vice President Hubert Humphrey, at a meeting in

Pittsburgh on May 13, 1965, said that "only the Vietcong has committed atrocities in Vietnam," he proved that American governmental propaganda had reached a degree of turpitude below which it
could not possibly sink.

IV.
Prophets of Certain Victory

In view of the triumph of Communism one might be tempted to call
American predictions of certain victory for "free" Vietnam—not to
mention claims that victory had already been achieved—a confirmation of the old pessimistic view that it is stupidity which determines
the fate of nations. Lack of understanding of the true meaning of
historical and military and political events was of course one reason
why so many prophets believed in the victory they were predicting.
But an equally important explanation was the political necessity of
justifying the war by assuring the American people that it was not
only just but also certain to be victorious. To say it was possible that
all these sacrifices might in the end turn out to have been in vain
would no doubt have created an anti-war movement strong enough
to put an end to American military intervention in Vietnam.

In the newspaper clippings and extracts from books and
magazines which I have collected I find at least fifty predictions of
certain victory over the Communists, made by prominent Americans between 1965 and 1972. (Many of these predictions can be
checked in Clyde Edwin Pettit's book *The Experts*.)

A small number of these pronouncements, which their authors
would surely like to be forgotten, will be sufficient:

"The Vietcong are going to collapse within weeks." (Walt Rostow to Daniel Ellsberg in July 1965, as quoted by David Halberstarn
in his book *The Best and Brightest*.)

"The Vietcong will just peter out." (General Maxwell Taylor,
October 27, 1966.)

The military editor of *The New York Times*, Hanson W. Baldwin,
wrote in his paper of December 26, 1967: "There seems to be little
reason to doubt that Hanoi has abandoned hope of conquering

South Vietnam." And another "expert," Admiral John S. McCoin, Jr., Commander in Chief, Pacific, in an interview with *Reader's Digest* of February 1969, stated concisely: "The enemy is beaten."

Although no American military leader had ever indicated that we were not winning, Admiral U. S. Grant Sharp and Secretary of Defense Robert McNamara stated, the first in October and the second in November, 1965: "We have stopped losing the war."

In the same vein, Vice President Hubert Humphrey assured the readers of *Newsweek* (November 8, 1965) that "the tide has turned. The Vietcong has been stopped." And in Saigon on February 10, 1966, Humphrey said: "There can be no doubt of our ultimate success."

This was also former President Eisenhower's conviction, who, in a speech at West Point on June 2, 1967, declared: "Whatever happens in Vietnam, I can see nothing but military victory." A believer in victory was of course also Richard Nixon, who stated on April 17, 1967 that "the defeat of the Communist forces in South Vietnam is inevitable." *Fortune* magazine in its issue of April, 1967 published an article about Vietnam under the somewhat premature title: "The War We've Won."

To show that the American people were given such assurances by many of the country's journalists, a good example is Joseph Alsop, of whom the book *The Experts* contains at least twenty predictions of impending victory. As early as April, 1961, Alsop wrote from Vietnam: "The good guys have been coming out on top for once." Almost a decade later, in December, 1970, he wrote that "victory has at last been won." *(Newsweek, December 7.)*

Some members of Congress, although far from doubting the wisdom of American involvement in Indochina, expressed themselves a little more cautiously. Gerald R. Ford, for instance, let it be known on February 23, 1971, that our overall objectives in Vietnam are being accomplished. And more than a year later, on April 17, 1972, Senator George Aiken said he was satisfied that the North Vietnamese are going to lose.

Apparently realizing that the war had not yet been won, but sure that it could not be lost, Gerald Ford stated on May 3, 1972: "Time is on our side."

V.
Supporters and Critics of the War

Apart from the firm supporters of the war, there are those whose later opposition to it made the public almost completely forget that they too supported President Johnson's policy of gradually increasing military intervention. But it remains important to emphasize that their later opposition to the Vietnam war was a service to the country.

One of the most consistent supporters of the war was Thomas J. Dodd, Democrat of Connecticut, who in a speech before the Senate on June 10, 1965, called those who favored the withdrawal of the United States from Vietnam not only "their own worst enemies," but also "enemies of decency." But, contrary to what most Americans remember about him, Robert Kennedy too opposed withdrawal. In a speech on May 6, 1965, he said that withdrawal "would involve a repudiation of commitments undertaken and confirmed by three administrations," adding in the style of men he would later firmly oppose: "We must show Hanoi that it cannot win the war."

His last statement of such support seems to have been what he said in an interview for *U. S. News and World Report* of March 14, 1966: "I favor continuing our military commitment." To pull out of Vietnam he considered "so unacceptable that it hardly needs to be discussed." But according to C. L. Sulzberger of *The New York Times* of February 22, 1966, Robert Kennedy had at that time not only begun to advocate a negotiated settlement of the war, but also taken the position that such a settlement should lead to the inclusion of Communists in the Saigon government.

How much Robert Kennedy had changed his mind about the war a year later became clear from an attack on him by President Johnson. According to *Time* magazine of March 17, 1967, Johnson told Kennedy: "If you keep talking like this, you won't have a political future in this country within six months . . . In six months all you doves will be destroyed."

Robert Kennedy's reference to "commitments" (a subject to be dealt with later on), reminds me of a similar statement by his brother Edward, who on A.B.C.'s program *Issues and Answers* on August 29, 1965, argued "that we have a commitment in South Vietnam," and that we "have to stand by our commitment." That the U. S. must fulfill its commitment with respect to Vietnam Senator Fulbright had already said several months before the arrival of the first U. S. combat troops at Danang on March 6, 1965.

It is comforting to learn that these transitory supporters and subsequent opponents of the war were at least from early 1967 joined in their opposition by an increasing number of colleagues in Congress, as well as by other respected Americans such a Professor Hans Morgenthau, columnist Walter Lippman, General James M. Gavin and former ambassadors George Kennan and John Kenneth Galbraith. It was Walter Lippman who, even before the first U. S. combat troops were sent to Vietnam, warned that Johnson was "on the verge of making the kind of ruinous historical mistake which . . . Hitler made when he attacked Russia." But this sort of warning made no more impression on the Administration, on Congress and on public opinion than did the memorable prediction of Ernest Gruening, Senator from Alaska, who according to the editorial of *Life* magazine of January 8, 1965, was, apparently before any other American leader, convinced that Vietcong victory was "ultimately inevitable."

How hesitatingly some Senators had gone along with what President Johnson decided had to be done to "save" South Vietnam for the so-called "free world" can be seen from a statement by Richard Nixon who, according to *U. S. News and World Report of* August 23, 1965, demanded of Johnson that top Senate Democrats be "disciplined" by their party, naming as the chief culprits Senators Fulbright and Mansfield.

VI.
Statements Hard to Believe

Senator Strom Thurmond, Democrat of South Carolina, on March 14, 1968, uttered the following warning to his fellow-Americans: "If we lose [in Vietnam] before you know it [the Communists] would be up the beaches of Hawaii."

Hanson W. Baldwin wrote in *The New York Times* Magazine of February 27, 1966: "If we cannot win the kind of war now being fought in Vietnam, then God help us, for we are undone throughout the world."

But did the U. S. really lose the war? Not according to President Nixon, who in a speech on February 20, 1973, at Columbia, South Carolina, told his audience three weeks after the signing of the Paris Cease-Fire, that the U. S. has "achieved peace with honor," which was our goal in Vietnam.

The Communist victory in South Vietnam, although in the final analysis due to political factors, was doubtless completed in April 1975 in the form of a military triumph over the U. S.-supported armed forces of the Saigon regime. To say in view of this fact that the U. S. has achieved its goal in Vietnam must sound today like one of the most nonsensical statements of the entire Second Indochina war. Putting a prophecy based on wishful thinking as though it were an established fact, Nixon came to his astonishing conclusion in this way: "What does peace with honor mean? The purpose of the U. S. involvement was not to conquer North Vietnam or obtain bases in South Vietnam or to acquire territory or domination over that part of the world." The purpose, Nixon explained, "was very simple: to prevent the imposition by force of a Communist government on the 17 million people of South Vietnam. That was our goal, and we achieved that goal, and we can be proud that we stuck it out until we reached that goal."

Another statement contrary to historical fact and combined with an indirect prophecy, was made earlier by General Maxwell Taylor, who wrote in *The New York Times* Magazine of October 1, 1967: "It is they [the Communist] who have started the war which cannot be won, and it is their leaders—not ours—who should be meditating upon the inevitability of failure."

No less ridiculous is what Major General Moshe Dayan of Israel said in a different context (according to *The Washington Post* of October 23, 1966): "The American army as a whole . . . gets satisfaction out of every day it spends in Vietnam . . . Most [soldiers] would volunteer for service in Vietnam if they were not posted there." The many deserters and the mass of young Americans who left their families and their country rather than fight in Vietnam will probably agree that ignorance is not a sufficient explanation for this statement. Dubious political motives alone can lead an otherwise normally intelligent person to say something which even the least informed American must recognize as being contrary to facts.

On the other hand, retired Air Force General Thomas D. White was not trying to lie but was merely revealing a lack of knowledge when he said, according to *Newsweek* of June 29, 1964: "We are [in Vietnam] to stop Communist China from obtaining the rice and other resources it must have if it is ever to become a world power."

The reason why China seems to do fairly well without the rice of Vietnam is simple. At the height of rice export from Vietnam and Cambodia under French colonial rule the total for the year 1937 was 2.2 million tons. China's yearly grain harvest in 1975 was 275 million tons. Official figures put the yearly harvest before 1950 at 108 million tons, a figure most experts consider too low. But even if pre-Communist China produced twenty or thirty million tons more, the increase since 1950 is at least twenty times the amount of the highest export figure for colonial Vietnam, while the difference between a good and a bad Chinese grain harvest can be as much as forty to fifty million tons, or again twenty times the amount of a possible surplus in Vietnam once the country's productivity is restored.

Something which, in view of the fact that most allies of the United States are glad we are at last out of Indochina, can be described only as another stupidity was a prediction made by Senator Thomas Dodd on December 7, 1967: "If the Administration were to negotiate a settlement that paved the way for an early Communist take-over, then it will mark the total eclipse of America as a great nation and the beginning of the end of the entire free world."

There is one last subject concerning the Second Indochina war which needs to be explained:

VII.
Costs and Casualties

On the basis of official statistics which are largely lacking on the Communist and highly unreliable on the American side, I shall try to answer the questions: which side spent more money on the Second Indochina war and which side killed more people?

The available figures prove that the United States spent a great deal more in Vietnam than Russia and China together, even during the final years that led to the collapse of the Saigon regime.

The figure of 160 billion dollars commonly cited as the cost of U. S. intervention in Indochina is not likely to give the average American an idea of the waste of taxpayers' money in a mistaken and essentially undemocratic foreign policy enterprise which would have been unjustified even if it had not been such an failure. (Somebody might readily figure out that this sum could have solved the serious financial problems of all major U. S. cities for at least twenty years.)

There are no reliable statistics to demonstrate in meaningful terms how the lives of many Americans could have been improved with the billions upon billions spent to kill more and more Vietnamese. According to *Time* magazine of January 22, 1965, the U. S. had already spent, before the bombing of the North and the arrival of our first combat troops, two million dollars a day, a sum which the magazine found "tolerable." But this sum rose rapidly during 1965. *The San Francisco Chronicle* reported on May 12, 1966: "The expenditure on artillery and mortar shells, machine gun and rifle bullets alone in Vietnam is seven million dollars a day." No wonder that by adding the seventy-five bombs it took our Air Force to produce one enemy corpse, Robert Sherrod calculated in *Life* magazine of January 27, 1967, that to kill one Communist soldier cost the United States no less than $400,000.

An imaginative New York teacher might one day charge his pupils to make the following calculations: How many days of shooting at Communist guerillas would equal the cost of maintaining full service at New York's Public Libraries and all museums for a whole year? And how much could have been done for education, health and urgent social services with the money it cost to kill one thousand enemies?

Even more expensive than the war on the ground was the air war. During the three years from February 1965 to March 1968, the bombing of North Vietnam (and secretly also of Laos) cost eight billion dollars.

As regards the assistance rendered to North Vietnam and indirectly to the Vietcong by the Soviet Union and China, fairly reliable estimates by U. S. intelligence services exist only for the period of 1970 to 1975. However, based on more or less accurate reports I collected over fifteen years, I am inclined to believe that the total cost of the Second Indochina war for the U. S. was close to ten times the amount spent by the Communists powers, and that Washington gave South Vietnam more than five times the amount Hanoi received from Moscow and Peking.

Three reports on aid to North and South Vietnam since 1970 seem to confirm this estimate. The New York Times of November 19, 1972 reported that U. S. aid to South Vietnam for the year 1971 was eighteen times as much as China gave during the same period to Hanoi, $1.37 billion against 75 million. Soviet aid to Hanoi was estimated by Senator Edward Kennedy (based on U. S. intelligence reports) to have been $100 million in 1971. The same reports supplied by the CIA and the State Department put U. S. aid to Saigon from 1970 to 1974 at more than 8 billion dollars, and although these were years of increasing Soviet and Chinese support for Hanoi, their combined aid to North Vietnam for the same period was put at less than one fourth of U. S. aid to Saigon.

The Indochina Resources Center in Washington—always critical of America's role in Indochina—reported on January 27, 1975 that the U. S. had spent well over 7 billion dollars since the cease-fire of January 1973, putting the aid to North Vietnam from China and

Russia at less than 1½ billion. Various newspaper reports after the fall of Saigon estimated that the South Vietnamese army surrendered more military equipment to the Communist troops during the month of April 1975 than the Chinese and Russians had sent to North Vietnam in two years.

The air war alone is said to have cost the U. S. more than 30 billion dollars, of which the more than 8,000 aircraft lost during the entire war probably accounted for nearly 10 billion. The *New York Post* of December 7, 1967, reported that between July 1965 and November 1967, no less than 1,630,000 tons of bombs had been dropped on North and South Vietnam, which amounted to 100 pounds of explosives for every person living in North and South Vietnam, and to 12 tons of bombs for every square mile of the country. These figures had risen two years later to 300 pounds of bombs for every man, woman and child, and to 22 tons for every square mile. Altogether, under Presidents Johnson and Nixon, 7 million tons had been dropped on Indochina, which was three times the amount dropped by the Allies during World War II on all enemy countries. Between late 1969 and August 1973, American planes dropped on Cambodia alone 250,000 tons of bombs—nearly three times the amount that fell on the British Isles in nearly six years of World War II. An Air War Study by the Cornell University Center for International Studies reported in 1973 that since Nixon took office, more bombs had been dropped on Indochina than the total of 2.9 million tons dropped during World War II and the Korean War combined.

In view of these figures it can hardly be surprising to learn that air attacks caused more victims among the people of Indochina than did the ground war. According to a New Jersey SANE report, eight years of bombing in North and South Vietnam resulted in 1½ million people killed, 3 million wounded and 9 million refugees. The fighting between the so-called "allied" and the Communist troops produced slightly fewer casualties. The available figures are: South Vietnamese killed 183,528; wounded 499,000; Vietcong and North Vietnamese killed 924,000 (the number of wounded is unknown); Americans killed 56,000; wounded 303,000.

The number of Communists killed can be accepted only with two reservations. First, nearly all American correspondents in Vietnam considered the official Saigon figures of enemy casualties as highly exaggerated; and second, these Saigon "body counts" comprised as a rule not only dead enemy soldiers but everyone, from old peasants to women and children, who died during the attempts by one side or the other to drive the enemy out of a village or town. *The New York Times* correspondent, Joseph Treaster, wrote in *Harper's Magazine* of July 1975: "One of the early measures of success, the body count, became such a ludicrous exercise in exaggeration by the Americans and South Vietnamese that we shall probably never know how many North Vietnamese and Vietcong were killed (or how many civilians lost their lives as the Americans sought more 'kills')."

However, due to the vast American and South Vietnamese superiority in fire power, which at times was as much as 10 to 1, the number of Communist soldiers killed and wounded was naturally much higher than that of the South Vietnamese and Americans. The total number of people killed in this conflict seems to be somewhere between 2½ and 3 million. The number of wounded must be close to 4 million, not counting the unknown number of wounded Communist soldiers, which may well be another 1½ million. Of the probably 3 million people killed during the entire war, a recent U. S. estimate puts the number of civilians at 1.4 million.

Compared with the figures of killed Communist and South Vietnamese soldiers, the number of U. S. soldiers killed and wounded is relatively small. Nevertheless, they were all wasted lives. I am sure it will not be long before most Americans will agree with General Daniel M. Shoup, who in May, 1966 said before a Los Angeles audience: "I want to tell you, I don't think that the whole of Southeast Asia, as related to the present and future safety and freedom of the people of this country, is worth the life and limb of a single American."

Quite obviously, America's political leadership, supported by a mostly well-meaning but constantly misled public, was hoping, from the beginning to just short of the calamitous end of U. S.

intervention in Vietnam, that our immense superiority in military resources would make victory certain. What our leaders from Truman to Nixon and Ford failed to realize was that in the essentially political struggle for Vietnam, victory depended not on the number of Communists we succeeded in killing, but on our ability to convince the South Vietnamese people that our aim was a nationally independent, politically free and socially progressive South Vietnam. It was sad enough that we did precisely the opposite of what was called for to successfully oppose the appeal of Communism in Vietnam. But much worse, in view of the likelihood of similar conflicts in the future, is the fact that our leaders still have not learned that in this kind of power struggle dollars and bombs are a poor substitute for constructive political ideas.

PART *Three*

The Turn of the Tide

I.
Why the War Did Not End in 1969

Many politically sophisticated authors have tried to answer the question why the United States continued the struggle to "save" South Vietnam in spite of increasing evidence that even with more than half a million American soldiers and the biggest air force in the world could not produce positive results.

This question first became really urgent in the spring of 1968, when it looked as though a political solution of the conflict had suddenly become possible. This is how I put it in my book *Vietnam: A Political History*, written in June 1968:

> Since December 1967, when the last chapter of this book was written, the fear expressed in its final paragraph (that the Vietnamese war would continue and might turn out to have been merely a prelude to World War III) has unexpectedly made way for the hope that a peaceful solution of the conflict may yet come about. This hope was aroused by President Johnson's announcement on March 31, 1968, that the bombing of North Vietnam would be significantly restricted and that he would not seek reelection.

I continued:

> The general reaction to the President's speech was that he had at last opened the road to peace negotiations with Hanoi. It was assumed in the

United States and abroad that the President no longer believed in the possibility of a military victory over the combined forces of the Vietcong and North Vietnamese, and that he had furthermore become aware of a change in American public opinion: More and more people apparently began to prefer a compromise solution to the prospect of several more years of inconclusive warfare.

This mood of the American people was only partly due to the political shock which the enemy's Tet Offensive of February 1968 had created in the United States. "The American people," I wrote,

were no longer inclined to believe the statements of men who had for years attempted to prove that all was going well with the war in Vietnam. Official optimism was discredited as never before, and propaganda based on it proved at least temporarily ineffective. The conclusion millions of Americans drew from the Tet Offensive was not so much that it had created an entirely new and highly critical situation; rather, it brought a sudden awareness that the situation had really always been critical—before the offensive as well as after it. The public had learned that the enemy had not been weakened by three years of massive military intervention, and became persuaded that he evidently could not be defeated at all. Almost over night, the Tet Offensive had wiped out the [optimistic] picture drawn by the Administration at the end of 1967, while emphatically confirming almost everything the critics of the Administration had been saying for the last three years.

In September 1975, a former CIA agent, Samuel Adams, revealed that in order to prevent the American press and public opinion from drawing erroneous conclusions about the chances the U. S. had of still winning the war, the forces of the enemy were reported by the CIA as being only half their real size.

Evidence of a drastic change in the public's mood after the Tet Offensive now came quite forcefully even from Congress—and not only from old opponents of the war such as Senator Albert Gore, who demanded on February 17, 1968, that the U. S. get out of the "morass of Vietnam," or Eugene McCarthy, whose success in the primaries of the 1968 presidential elections was due to his opposition to the war. Robert F. Kennedy, too, became more outspoken, calling what America was doing in Vietnam "immoral and intolerable," while Mike Mansfield, warning against further escalation, stated: "We are in the wrong place and we are fighting the wrong war."

What Americans were able to learn about Vietnam from such veteran correspondents as Robert Shaplen of *The New Yorker* and Charles Mohr of *The New York Times* made them reject the claim of our military leaders that the Tet Offensive supplied only new evidence of the enemy's inevitable defeat. The unsuccessful campaign for another 200,000 American troops proved conclusively that our generals' ability to deceive the American public was obviously declining, even if their capacity to deceive themselves remained unimpaired.

Negotiations aiming at a compromise solution of the war started in Paris on May 13, 1968. Four years later, Americans were still fighting in Vietnam, and the United States was continuing to support another three years of war, accepting, as Charles Frankel put it, "its cruelty, its cost, its shame, its obtuse persistence in folly," (as quoted by James Reston in *The New York Times* of August 10, 1975).

The war not only continued (in spite of the withdrawal of American troops starting in June 1969); it was even enlarged by the invasion of Cambodia on April 30, 1970, and by the large-scale resumption of the bombing of North Vietnam. The total amount of bombs dropped under President Nixon in the three years from 1969 through 1971 was higher than under Johnson from 1965 to 1968.

Few would now deny that the agreement, which after nearly five years of on-and-off negotiations was signed at Paris on January 27, 1973, could have been obtained by Nixon in 1969. No one will ever know why he rejected it in 1969. No doubt, there was, as Anthony Lewis put it, "arrogance in the pursuit of folly." And it is also possible that Nixon was convinced that through sheer persistence he might do what Johnson had failed to accomplish.

But if Nixon, after being elected President in 1968, failed to grasp his chance to pull the United States out of Vietnam as honorably as he could hope to at the time, he had no new or original reasons for continuing the war. He did so for essentially the same reasons that had prompted four administrations to lead the country, step by step, into what had become the morass of Vietnam, reasons that had prevented his predecessors from breaking with the course initiated under Truman when the United States came to the support of the French war of colonial reconquest.

In dealing with something as complex as America's involvement in Vietnam it will be hard to provide explanations based on sound reasoning that will ever become generally accepted. But much of what has been said by informed critics of our Vietnam policy deserves consideration.

Alastair Buchan wrote in *Foreign Affairs* of July 1975: "One may legitimately ask why the United States became and remained so preoccupied with resistance to Communist penetration in an area where it had few economic and no direct strategic interests." And with a caution that has always been the hallmark of serious political criticism he says: "Clearly, the answer is in part ideological." Indeed, there has never been a time in American history when ideological obsessions marred so disastrously our leaders' political judgment.

Others have tried to answer the question why our leaders, after at least some of them had realized that the aims of the U. S. in Vietnam were unrealizable, still persisted in their hopeless pursuit. One reason was surely fear of how the public would react to an admission of failure after having been told for years that not only the so-called freedom of South Vietnam but even our security would be threatened if the Communists were not defeated in Vietnam. That this fear could not be substantiated made it seem no less real.

One expression of that fear was Johnson's remark (reported by Tom Wicker in his *JFK and LBJ*): "I am not going to be the President who saw Southeast Asia go the way China went." John K. Fairbank undoubtedly had in mind this fear of our leaders when he gave as one of the reasons for Washington's stubborn perseverance in its policy of "saving" South Vietnam "that a loss of a foreign country would be disastrous for the party in power."

Nixon too seemed to be obsessed by this fear. On October 10, 1969, he told Republican Party leaders at Camp David: "I am not going to be the first American President who loses a war." When I quoted this remark during a lecture at Southern Illinois University, one student commented: "If there had not been a Vietnam war, which Nixon worked so hard to bring about, he would today not be in the predicament of being the first American President to lose a war."

These domestic political considerations, in the case of Nixon, were summed up by Stuart Hampshire, the British critic of U. S. policy in Vietnam, as follows: "The American involvement in the war in Indochina was prolonged after 1968 principally for electoral reasons." Fear of losing an election if they admitted the failure of our Vietnam policy and gave up the effort to "save" South Vietnam was no doubt one of the chief reasons why four consecutive administrations persisted in this ill-advised course.

As the American people grew more tired of the war—its costs, its casualties and its damage to the reputation of their country—it became more urgent (but also more difficult) to explain why the war had to be continued. This is the reason why American propaganda, in spite of its declining credibility, continued all the stale references to Communist aggression, defense of freedom, and certain victory, with increasing emphasis on one argument that has even survived the end of the war.

According to this particular argument, in which the defense of alleged national interests was tied up with imperatives of political morality, the U. S. was in Vietnam because we had "a promise to keep," or, to put it in its more common political terms, "to fulfill a commitment made to an ally." Both aspects of this argument were concisely expressed by President Nixon when he said in a speech on November 3, 1969: "A nation cannot remain great if it betrays its allies and lets down its friends."

As to the veracity of this claim, repeated dozens of times, between 1964 and 1975 by administration spokesmen and other defenders of U. S. military intervention in Vietnam, I would quote former President Eisenhower, who in a press conference on August 17, 1965, stated: "But I think there was no commitment ever given in a military context that we are going . . . to do anything in a military way." (*The Experts*, p. 234) It had been Eisenhower himself, however, who, after the Geneva Agreement of July 1954, acted as if such a commitment to an ally existed, ignoring a real American commitment made at the end of the Geneva Conference, when our chief delegate stated that the U. S. would neither threaten nor use force to upset the agreement.

More important is that Secretary of State Henry Kissinger, immediately after the collapse of the Saigon regime on April 30, 1975, put the blame on Congress, which he said had not lived up to an American commitment to come to the rescue of the Saigon regime, thus implying that such a commitment had been made to President Thieu before the signing of the Paris Accord of January 1973. "Congress, meanwhile," wrote *The New Yorker* of May 5, 1975, "was learning of this new commitment for the first time, and was surprised at being accused of not having upheld a promise it did not know the United States had made." As I have written elsewhere, "the United States entered the war under the pretext that it had an obligation to come to the aid of an endangered ally, in total disregard of the fact that this ally was a mere creature of the United States and would not have existed if the Americans had not intervened in Indochina after the retreat of the French." (*A Dragon Defiant*, pp. 116–17)

This is how Professor Hans Morgenthau, one of the most effective critics of our Vietnam policy, put the same argument after the total failure of our policy had become evident: "We could never have committed ourselves to Diem or Thieu if we had not first put them into a position as recipients of our commitments," adding that these regimes "either owed their very existence or at least their temporary survival to America's intervention." This created what Morgenthau calls "the fraudulent character of the relationship [between the U. S. and South Vietnam], making a Quisling regime play the role of a sovereign government."

It is just not true that we came to the aid of a viable regime threatened by subversion and aggression. The truth is that we ourselves created and then sustained a non-viable regime, for the purpose of being able to intervene and to call our intervention assistance for an ally.

For Americans eager to know the truth about this tragic episode in our history, nothing seems more important today than to realize that, if the United States had not gone back on its word at Geneva that it would not interfere with the agreement concluded between France and the government of Ho Chi Minh our so-called ally in South Vietnam would certainly not have existed after July 1956, and the Second Indochina war, during which we nearly destroyed the country we claimed to be saving, would never have taken place.

II.
U. S. Withdrawal and Vietnamization

Opposition to the war—nourished primarily by reports of U. S. casualties, loss of planes and growing numbers of pilots captured over North Vietnam—became ever more vocal among America's youth, in Congress and even in conservative parts of the nation, including some of the business community. As early as March 1968, *Newsweek*, which had for some time been disenchanted with the war, quoted approvingly the following rather sensational statement from *The Wall Street Journal:* "We think the American people should be getting ready to accept, if they haven't already, the prospect that the Vietnam effort may be doomed."

The fact that Nixon, six months after assuming office, began the withdrawal of U. S. troops from Vietnam, shows better than any anti-war statements or listing of anti-war demonstrations, how rapidly opposition to the war was growing after the Spring of 1968. For years, suggestions of withdrawal had been denounced as giving aid to the enemy. Dr. Henry Kissinger wrote in *Look* magazine of August, 1966, "withdrawal would be disastrous," and our former Chief Delegate to the United Nations, Daniel P. Moynihan, attacked what he called "liberals" in *U. S. News and World Report* of October 9, 1967, for proposing that we get out of Vietnam. (I tried vainly to find any condemnation of Nixon for beginning withdrawal in 1969—a demand of anti-war groups which only a year earlier was still being forcefully denounced.)

How tired the American people had become of the war— something of which Nixon must have been keenly aware—became evident in the country's sense of relief with the troop withdrawals.

The first news came in June 1969. Of the 541,000 American soldiers stationed in South Vietnam in March 1969, only 69,000 were left by May 1, 1972.

Reminiscing about this period, Maynard Parker wrote in an article in *Foreign Affairs* of January 1975:

Although millions of Americans were sincerely and genuinely outraged by the brutality of the Vietnamese War, the Nixon Administration, and particularly Secretary of Defense Laird, realized that the vast majority of the Americans were opposed to the war not because of any moral concern over what was happening in Vietnam, but because they did not want their sons to die in the rice fields of Vietnam. Accordingly, the Administration correctly deduced that if it could lower both the draft calls and the weekly American killed-in-action (KIA) casualty figures, they could take much steam out of the anti-war movement.

It may never be known whether this policy was initiated (and guardedly pursued for three years) because Nixon and his entourage recognized that a military solution of the conflict in favor of the Saigon regime had become impossible. But even if this had been recognized—which I doubt was the case—it could never have been admitted. To admit this would have amounted to a confession that what the U. S. was doing in Vietnam had been wrong from the beginning, something our responsible leaders refuse to do even today.

Reasons other than the impossibility of victory had to be advanced to explain why it was now right to do what had been called, during the preceding four years, a betrayal of the "free world." Since domestic political considerations forced Nixon to begin withdrawing troops, while he and his advisers still remained unable to conceive of, let alone admit, the possibility of failure, what the Administration said to explain this new policy surprised neither its supporters nor its opponents. Troops were now withdrawn, the American people were told, not because the military situation had become hopeless but for a better reason: the situation had improved so much that to defeat aggression now required fewer and in the end probably no American troops at all.

This was called the "Vietnamization" of the war, which Hannah Arendt pertinently called "a public relations slogan to excuse the evacuation of American troops," adding as an additional reason for the urgency of this evacuation the fact that our troops, because they were "ridden by drugs, corruption, desertions and plain rebellion, could no longer be left there." (Bicentennial Address at Boston on May 20, 1975, as published by *The New York Review of Books*, June 26, 1975.)

The American public was expected to believe that the South Vietnamese army would now be able to do alone what it had failed to do with the help of over half a million American troops in four years of common effort: defeat the Communists militarily. Victory continued to be proclaimed as no less certain than ever, although the slow pace of Nixon's troop withdrawal, the continuation and even increase of bombing the North, as well as the delivery of more military hardware to the South Vietnamese army seemed to indicate doubts about the ultimate success of "Vietnamization." But if such doubts existed, they found no expression in anything the Administration continued to say about the war.

For opponents of the war, this optimism was explicable after 1968 only in one of two possible ways: either its exponents had reached a high degree of irrational self-deception or they recognized that to defend their policy made it absolutely necessary to claim that victory remained certain even if this required more lies than ever. Wishful thinking no doubt distorted the perception of reality (never very acute in regard to Vietnam) of many American political and military leaders; but there were enough who, although privately questioning their professed optimism (Dr. Kissinger was one of them), considered it their duty to say the situation in Vietnam was hopeful, even if this required a certain contempt for the American people's intelligence. Nor was this really new. For years they had been trained to believe that the Vietcong had little support in South Vietnam, while our frequent killing of civilians was usually defended by claiming that all the victims had been supporting the Vietcong.

The idea that the South Vietnamese army would win the war

had been propagated before the massive American military intervention in the Spring of 1965. General William Westmoreland, for years U. S. Commander in Vietnam, said in April, 1964 that it was "inconceivable that the Vietcong could ever defeat the armed forces of South Vietnam," an opinion still shared at that time by Under Secretary of State George W. Ball, who on ABC's program *Issues and Answers* (May 10, 1964) said "the biggest asset on our side [was] the demonstrated will of the South Vietnamese people to fight," which even before the collapse of the Saigon army in March and April 1975 had always been truer of those Vietnamese who fought on the other side—something Ball himself had recognized by the summer of 1965.

Although insisting that in the end the Communists would be defeated, few defenders of Nixon's strategy were firm in expressing confidence in Vietnamization. Only people who will long be remembered for the many wrong predictions they made expressed satisfaction with Vietnamization. One of these was Joseph Alsop, who as early as September, 1969 said that it was going well indeed, so well that he was able to say in his *Newsweek* report of December 1970: "The object of our long agony in Vietnam . . . has been achieved . . ." Faithful to his journalistic technique of persuasion through exaggeration, he referred again, as late as April, 1972 to the "triumphant success of President Nixon's Vietnamization program."

This was of course also the belief of President Thieu, who in an interview with Oriana Fallaci said that Vietnamization worked marvelously, and that everything has worked out as he expected (*L'Europeo*, December 30, 1972). But whereas for Joseph Alsop victory had already been won at the end of 1972, Thieu, in January 1970, merely predicted that it "will come in two or three years when the Communists are completely defeated."

Another believer was Secretary of Defense Melvin Laird, who, after a visit to South Vietnam in February 1970 saw positive progress in Vietnamization—apparently the only prominent spokesman for the Administration who still called Vietnamization even two years later (in June 1972) "astonishingly successful." And three weeks before the signing of the Paris cease-fire of January 1973 he repeated: "The South Vietnamese are now capable of defending themselves."

Optimism, whether or not based on the belief that Vietnamization was working well, was unaffected by the withdrawal of more and more U. S. troops, whose number had been reduced between June 1969 and March 1971 from 541,000 to 248,000. The Democratic Speaker of the House of Representatives, Carl Albert, for instance, said on July 2, 1971: "Mr. Nixon is optimistic and I think optimism is well founded." One wonders whether he and other U.S. leaders who shared his opinion had given any thought to what Walter Lippman had written in *Newsweek* of November 5, 1969: "This must be just about the first time in the history of warfare that a nation has thought it could prevail by withdrawing troops and reducing its military presence."

Reasons for the failure of Vietnamization as a way of winning the war are pertinently given in an article by Joseph B. Treaster in *Harpers* Magazine of July, 1975 entitled "The Fraud of Vietnamization." Treaster, who spent five years in Vietnam as a reporter for *The New York Times*, believes that a major reason for the low fighting spirit of the South Vietnamese soldiers and the failure of Vietnamization was the corruption among the army leadership. "As billions of American dollars gushed into Vietnam, the military became the most corrupt as well as the most influential institution in the country." While the generals lived in luxury, the South Vietnamese soldier "was paid a pittance, stood little chance of being promoted without bribing someone," besides knowing that his wife and children lacked sufficient food, decent housing and badly needed medical care—facts which Americans in leadership positions in Vietnam either refused to recognize or to admit as detrimental to the morale of the South Vietnamese army.

This alone would have led to the failure of Vietnamization, to which, as Treaster put it, "Lies were the inevitable response. As the situation became more desperate, the lies became more blatant." Going further, Treaster thinks that "what doomed the American venture in Vietnam was an addiction to lies and deception."

Confirming Treaster's explanation of the failure of Vietnamization, John Kenneth Galbraith wrote in *The New York Times* of July 12, 1975, that almost none of our leaders "could grasp the most elementary political proposition that men will not die to sustain the greed and graft of others."

This, among other political reasons, makes it necessary to take a closer look at the corruption prevalent under every South Vietnamese regime from Diem to Thieu.

III.
The Debilitating Effect of Corruption

As I wrote in my book *A Dragon Defiant*, based on a report in *The New York Times* of November 13, 1966,

Rule by force was accomplished by widespread corruption in the administration from top to bottom. Corruption, it was reported by informed American observers, was taking no less than 40 per cent of U. S. aid to South Vietnam. The beneficiaries of this corruption were not only contractors, high administrators, landlords, generals and intermediary agents between business and government, but also lower officials in the administration who extracted bribes from any citizen for whatever service he may have needed or had a right to receive. Those rich enough were able to get exemption from military service for their sons or permission for them to study abroad, for which sums as high as $10,000 were paid.

We supported leaders, Robert Shaplen wrote, "amenable to doing things 'our way,' no matter how corrupt and ineffective they and their entourage might be."

Time magazine of June 5, 1968 reported that anyone who paid $25,000 could be made chief of a province, calling this "an investment quickly earned back via shakedown of the local population and kickbacks on licenses or shipments of goods." A few years later Joseph Treaster reported the price for which high administrators sold these positions had risen to $50,000. "At the top," Treaster said, "graft-taking generals set the tone for a moral rot that ate into every corner of society." For an example, he mentions Nguyen Van Toan, commonly called "the cinnamon general" who, by monopolizing the profitable cinnamon trade in the provinces he controlled, was said to have made millions of dollars. After raping a fifteen-year old girl he had to be dismissed, but early in 1975 he was made commander of the vital military region that encompassed Saigon. Thus it was a man of the sort of character common among thieves and rapists who was in charge of defending the South Vietnamese capitol until it fell to the advancing Communist troops.

Toi Boa Ga, a publication of the Vietnamese Resources Center at Cambridge, Mass. reported in its issue of July-August, 1974 that money and 2,200 sacks of rice sent to flood victims in the province of Phu Bon never reached these victims but was shared among the high officials of the province. And land belonging to sixty families of disabled veterans, widows and orphans of former soldiers in the province of Tuyen Duc was taken from them by officials and landlords, who threatened the legal owners with murder if they insisted on getting their land back. The same publication also reported that high governmental officials usurped and fenced off 450,000 acres of forest land in order to pocket the millions in profits from logging exports.

One aspect of life in South Vietnam is not usually associated with corruption but, like corruption, was no doubt one of the reasons why the mass of peasants could not be mobilized against the Vietcong. This was the Thieu regime's way of handling the vital problem of land reform which, with American aid, was undertaken in 1970 as a political effort to gain popular support for the Thieu regime. William Hazeltine reported in a letter to *The New York Times* of December 7, 1971 that the regime's claim of having distributed 500,000 acres of land to peasants was a pure swindle. "The land in secure areas has been distributed not to the landless but rather by the landlords themselves to their own relatives to escape the provisions of the law." (Hazeltine's letter was signed also by Jean Doyle and Michael Ryan of the Committee of Concerned Asian Scholars at Cambridge, Mass.) For more details on Thieu's so-called land reform, see the article "Land Reform in Vietnam Reversed in Some Areas," by David K. Shipler (*The New York Times*, January 14, 1974).

"Absentee landlords are still riding with pacifying troops," wrote

The Washington Evening Star of March 31, 1967, based on a report of the *London Times*. They do this "not merely to grab back their land but to extort back rents for the time they had fled from the Vietcong."

In some areas, reported *The New York Times*, February 25, 1974, Thieu's land reform program of 1970 was systematically reversed. If the areas became secure, the old landowners returned to reclaim land they had abandoned because of the war, and with the help of corrupt local officials forced the peasants to relinquish the land they had been given—some by the Vietcong—just a few years ago. Thousands of peasants who had regarded themselves as owners of their land became tenants again, forced again to pay rents up to 60 per cent of the crop—one of the main reasons why even among villagers who had no love for the Communists, the Thieu regime, in the crucial period of March and April 1975, could nowhere count on any kind of popular support.

Shocking details about corruption, especially among generals and high government officials, were made public during the last years of the Thieu regime, by Reverend Tran Hu Thanh, a Catholic priest who claimed that in his fight against corruption in South Vietnam he had the tacit approval of the Vatican, which may have been the reason why Thieu, perhaps the country's leading corruptionist, did not dare to throw Thanh into prison.

According to Nguyen Van Ngai, minister of rural development until he was ousted in 1974, Thieu left Vietnam not as a poor refugee like so many of his countrymen, but as a billionaire. He and others, among them Prime Minister Tran Thieu Khiem, became rich by "misuse of state-controlled monopolies on import and export, siphoning off millions from American aid and under the Vietnamization program" (*The New York Times*, May 11, 1975). Some of these South Vietnamese leaders tried to ship several tons of gold to Zurich, Switzerland when they recognized that the rotten regime which had made them rich would soon collapse.

More details on corruption by the rapist General Nguyen Van Toan can be found in an article in *The New York Times* Magazine of May 25, 1975 by Fox Butterfield, for years one of America's best-

informed reporters on Vietnam. General Toan not only profited
from the cinnamon trade, but also collected bribes from highland
woodcutters, and was involved in the profitable drug business. Officers under him as well as under other generals sold drugs to soldiers at military outposts. Some of these officers too are said to have
amassed huge fortunes.

These and similar stories about corruption, which I collected
during my last visit to South Vietnam in April, 1973, were widely
known and generally believed by the suffering people, and, as
Joseph Treaster put it, "they pervaded the moral fabric of the country." An army colonel quoted by Fox Butterfield in *The New York
Times* of May 28, 1975, connected the corruption with the rebellious
behavior of the soldiers when the army collapsed by saying: "Under
our system, the generals amassed riches for their families, but soldiers got nothing and saw no moral sanction in their leadership. In
the end they took their revenge."

According to *The New York Times* of October 19, 1972, even
former Vice President Nguyen Cao Ky, after having been kicked
out of the inner circle which had access to American money, accused
Thieu and his collaborators of being corrupt, hoping no doubt that
the stories about his own abuses would be forgotten. One of these
stories I learned while working on this book in July 1975 in Aspen,
Colorado. In a letter to *The Denver Post* of July 23, 1975, a man by
the name of Kenneth J. Naysmith of Lakewood, Colorado, wrote:
"In mid-1970 I returned from a year in Vietnam, where I lived near
a 10,000 man airbase being rented by the United States, not from
the needy Vietnamese people or government, but from Madame Ky,
wife of the Vice President of South Vietnam." And confirming with
a typical example that corruption was widespread also at the lowest
governmental levels, Naysmith continued: "Outside my offices in
Saigon a Vietnamese man on a motorbike veered in front of a U. S.
truck and was killed, and when the police arrived, they asked the
innocent American driver how much he would give them to let him
go."

(For more details on corruption before it got worse under Thieu,
see David Halberstam in *Harpers* magazine of December, 1967.)

Because of the similarities in regard to corruption between South Vietnam and Cambodia, I want to add here what Sydney H. Schanberg wrote in *The New York Times* of November 24, 1974 about corruption in pre-Communist Cambodia:

The sons of generals drive Alfa Romeos and Cougar fastbacks. The governor of a province is known to sell ammunition and drugs to the enemy. Other government officials can be seen selling automatic rifles and uniforms to wealthy merchants, who in turn sell them to both sides. Low-salaried colonels—some accused of pocketing the payrolls of their units—build luxurious villas here in the capital [Phnom Penh] and rent them to Americans for $700 a month.

"At the other end of the scale," Schanberg adds, "hundreds of thousands of Cambodian refugees uprooted by the fighting and jammed into Phnom Penh often cannot afford to buy enough rice."

What George McT. Kahin revealed about General Lon Nol, who with CIA support overthrew Prince Sihanouk, is probably the most shocking story of corruption that has come out of Southeast Asia since the beginning of the struggle for Indochina. This American protege, playing his role up to his fall on April 17, 1975, is said to have been, before he assumed power, engaged as middleman in very lucrative arms smuggling for the Vietcong, something Sihanouk vainly tried to stop. One wonders whether Lon Nol became a henchman for the Americans only because he found it more profitable than to continue smuggling arms for the Vietcong.

Nixon's policy of continuing the war, which had already cost 130 billion dollars and nearly 50,000 American lives by 1969, enabled these crooks, more numerous in South Vietnam than in Cambodia, to continue filling their pockets and foreign bank accounts with American taxpayers' money.

Nobody should be surprised if Americans, once the shocking facts of corruption in South Vietnam become general knowledge, will see some kind of historical justice in the failure of our policy to "save" one of the most rotten regimes of this century.

PART *Four*

The Hard Road To Peace

I.
Why Peace Was Not "at Hand"

After four years of so-called negotiations at Paris, followed by several months of secret talks between Henry Kissinger and the Hanoi delegate Le Duc Tho during the late summer and early fall of 1972, Kissinger announced on October 26 that peace was finally "at hand." Obviously wanting the American people to believe that this was really the case, President Nixon said in a speech in Michigan two days later: "Vietnam being over, we are proud that our trips to Peking and Moscow paved the way not just for ending this war but for a generation of peace"—implying that the war was over because he had succeeded in persuading the Chinese and Russians to pressure Hanoi into agreeing to a peaceful solution of the conflict.

If it seemed so important for Nixon in October, 1972, shortly before the presidential elections, to create the impression that he had fulfilled earlier promises to end the war, the reason can only be his awareness of the strength of the opposition to the war. Presenting himself as the architect of a peace now strongly desired by the American people no doubt greatly improved Nixon's chances of being re-elected.

This important consideration prevented Nixon and Kissinger from denying Hanoi's claim that the agreement to end the war was ready for signing on October 31. Although peace was *not* at hand, as

we now know, because Washington had failed to get Saigon's consent to the text of the agreement concluded with Hanoi, Kissinger
still tried to give the opposite impression by saying that Hanoi's
report about it was "on the whole a fair account." The agreement, he
also said, was 99 per cent complete. Not wanting to admit that it
could not be signed because of President Thieu's refusal to do so,
Washington gave the fact that a few minor problems had to be
settled—"basically linguistic and technical details"—as the only reason why the signing had to be postponed.

It is now well-established that Nixon, prior to his expected re-
election, did not want the American people to know what he knew
very well: the war was far from "being over." To put it bluntly, the
war was not over because Nixon's underling Thieu had vetoed the
peace. Nixon continued to mislead the American people about the
chances of peace by repeating, only four days before the election,
that "we have reached a substantial agreement."

The most significant provision of the agreement, as it became
known at the end of January, 1973, was the prospect that the South
Vietnamese Communists would participate legally in their country's
political life. That this was unacceptable to Thieu did not surprise
anyone acquainted with the real views of this dictator. Thieu had
made this clear long before he became a one-man candidate for
president and was confirmed as such in the totalitarian elections of
October, 1971. On August 27, 1968, Thieu said in a speech at Bien
Hoa: "I would never accept any Communist to run in an election in
Vietnam." And as if he were already anticipating a time when
Nixon might be willing to accept a compromise solution of the war,
Thieu said on September 26, 1969: "We will not stop short of
victory, no matter what happens in Washington." Knowing quite
well how fervently most Vietnamese desired an end to the war, he
stated in Saigon on July 15, 1970: "We will beat to death the people
who are demanding immediate peace." And angrily disregarding
Nixon's insinuation prior to his re-election that he had kept his
promise to end the war, Thieu said on October 27, 1972, one day
after Kissinger's claim that peace was "at hand": "A cease-fire can

come only when I myself take a pen and sign the agreement." This alone proves what the *New Republic* said in an editorial of May 5, 1975: that Nixon had given Thieu veto power over the Paris peace negotiations.

It was Thieu's veto which, between November 7, 1972, and the signing of the cease-fire on January 27, 1973, not only produced a new tidal wave of American lies about Vietnam but also led to a resumption of terror-bombing over North Vietnam on a hitherto unknown scale, leading to anti-American demonstrations all over the world and to numerous protests by governments of many allies of the United States. (For details, see my article "Vietnam: Truce Without Peace" in the Spring, 1973, issue of *Dissent.*)

The purpose of these new lies was to hide the fact that serious trouble had arisen between Washington and Saigon, a fact well-known to Kissinger and Nixon when they made their respective pre-election statements implying that the end of the war was near. It was of course impossible for them to confess that their efforts had been thwarted by a man who, in the absence of U. S. support, would have lost power within a week. Their only choice was to blame Hanoi for the embarrassing fact that the "99 per cent complete" agreement was not being signed. In the face of Hanoi's repeated willingness to sign immediately what had been agreed upon in October, Washington reached a new low of credibility in the world by claiming that additional demands raised by the Communist side stood in the way of immediate peace.

Negotiations between Washington and Hanoi, resumed on November 20, 1972, were recessed on November 25, again taken up on December 7, only to be broken off again on December 13, no doubt because Washington, in deference to Thieu, no longer accepted what it had agreed upon in October. On December 16, Kissinger, charging Hanoi with procrastination, said "the deal is off," apparently not realizing what his remark implied: that at one time a deal had been "on." Two days later the so-called Christmas-bombing of North Vietnam was started, decided upon by Nixon.

The true reasons for the Christmas bombing could of course not

be admitted. Tom Wicker (*The New York Times* April 22, 1975) referring to Kissinger's announcement that peace was "at hand," and to
Thieu's explanation in his resignation speech of why he had to reject
what had been agreed upon in October, remarked: "This is almost
entirely contrary to the official version given the American people,
who were told that Hanoi had to be forced to keep its word by the
so-called 'carpet-bombing' of Christmas, 1972." Trying to give the
true reasons for this universally condemned bombing, I wrote in my
article in *Dissent* "Truce Without Peace": "Once Nixon could claim
that his bombing had forced Hanoi to resume negotiations and submit to his conditions, he felt free to use whatever pressure was
needed to make Thieu accept the cease-fire thus obtained."

U. S. planes, the Pentagon reported according to a Wire Service
Dispatch from Washington on January 17, 1973, bombarded Indochina with 95,490 tons of bombs in December, again almost as
great a tonnage as Hitler had dropped on the British Isles during the
entire World War II. In the first two days alone (according to *The
New York Times* of December 22, 1972), an estimated 20,000 tons had
been dropped, the equivalent of the Hiroshima atomic bomb. "In
densely populated suburbs of Hanoi and Haiphong," I wrote, "as
well as in smaller towns, several thousand civilians were killed or
wounded. Whole districts of Hanoi, including schools, apartment
houses, and the city's main hospital were smashed to bits by a type
of carpet bombing that surpassed most of the terror bombings in
World War II."

The highly respected French anti-Nazi writer Vercors said after
the Christmas bombing that the U. S. was "transposing an entire
land into a lunar landscape." Many Europeans and probably also
Americans understood what Vercors—in a state of true political despair about America—said about Nixon and the Pentagon: "They
feel they are masters of the world" and they do "worse than Hitler
without risking his fate." (*The New York Times* January 5, 1973) How
the people in England felt, Alistair Buchan revealed when he wrote
in the *London Times* at the end of December 1972 about "the anger
and contempt which President Nixon's area bombing in North
Vietnam aroused in this country."

What the American public did not learn at the time was that even

some members of the U. S. airforce in Vietnam were morally outraged by the resumption of bombing after they had been led to
expect that the war was about to end. To prevent this embarrassing
fact from becoming known, crew pilots and members who refused to
go on these new missions were quietly sent home.

Nixon was reported to be deeply aggrieved by what he considered unfair criticism, especially in Europe where nobody seemed to
accept his attempts to justify the Christmas bombing. On the contrary, when Nixon claimed that he had ordered it because Hanoi
had to be forced to sign a cease-fire, this was regarded by most
Europeans as another lie. The highly respected French newspaper
Le Monde, whose editors apparently knew quite well that it was not
Hanoi but Thieu who refused to sign a cease-fire agreement, wrote
on December 21, 1972: "If [Nixon] dared to go to the very end of his
logic, he should now bomb Saigon."

To be sure, many American shared the feeling about the
Christmas bombing which *The New Leader* of January 22, 1973 expressed in an article entitled "The Shame of Richard Nixon." But
critics of our Vietnam policy rightly deplore that so many Americans still fail to recognize how much of what Nixon and Kissinger
said to justify the Christmas bombing consisted again merely of lies,
not to mention what they continued to say to justify our involvement in Indochina. Anthony Lewis, for instance, put the matter
well when he wrote in *The New York Times* of January 1975: "The
interesting question is not why Henry Kissinger says what he does
about Indochina but why anyone goes on believing him." This,
unfortunately, is true even today, after events have proved that
almost everything Kissinger said about the Vietnamese war during
the last three years has been either mistaken or a distortion of fact.

II.
The Paris Agreement

The agreement to end the war, finally signed in Paris on January 27,
1973, must be recognized in spite of its strongly emphasized military
character of a "cease-fire," as primarily a political treaty. It was

aimed not only at ending the war but also at settling the political future of South Vietnam. It even envisioned the reunification of the South and North, "to be carried out step by step through peaceful negotiations." (Chapter V, Article 15 of the cease-fire agreement).

The essentially political character of the agreement was made evident beyond all doubt by Chapter I, Article I, which is a brief but highly important introduction to the long text. What it says proves that not Saigon and Washington, but Hanoi and the South Vietnamese Communists, had achieved their goal. "The United States and all other countries respect the independence, sovereignty, unity and territorial integrity of Vietnam as recognized by the 1954 Geneva Agreements on Vietnam"—precisely what the Vietcong and Hanoi had been fighting for since the United States prevented the all-Vietnamese elections of 1956 for the unification of Vietnam.

The specifics concerning the political settlement of the conflict, contained in Articles 9, 10, 11, and 12, provided for a "National Council of National Reconciliation and Concord," consisting not only of the Saigon government and the Communists (always referred to as the "two parties"), but also of representatives of the non-Communist so-called Third Force. The task of this council was described as implementation of this agreement through the "insurance of democratic liberties" and the organizing of "free and democratic elections provided for in Article 9." All of this the two parties were supposed to accomplish within 90 days. The democratic liberties were listed in Article II as freedom of the press, freedom of assembly, freedom of organization and freedom of political activities, none of which existed in South Vietnam.

If taken seriously, what Articles 9, 10, 11 and 12 contained could mean only that everybody, including the Communists, would now be able to participate legally in the political life of South Vietnam and also in the elections to be organized by the National Council of National Reconciliation and Concord.

These political provisions alone make quite plausible why the chief negotiator of the Communists, Le Duc Tho, called the Paris accord a very great victory for his side. The struggle for power in South Vietnam was now supposed to be fought in the arena of politics, where the Vietcong had its greatest strength. Hanoi had achieved near victory, not as Joseph Alsop wrote on November 1, 1972, "accepted near total defeat."

Ironically, freedom, democracy, self-determination of the South Vietnamese people for the defense of which the U. S. claimed to have gone to war, were now supposed to come about as a concession to the undefeated Communists, necessary to get the U. S. out of a war which it had failed to win.

But there were still other, equally important reasons why the Communists accepted the Paris accord with such demonstrative satisfaction. Article 5 of the Cease-Fire Agreement stipulated that all U. S. and so-called allied forces be withdrawn from South Vietnam within 60 days, which meant that one of the most important goals of the Communists—to get all Americans and other foreign troops out of Vietnam, had been achieved.

No less important was that among the military provisions of the cease-fire, no mention was made of the Hanoi troops in South Vietnam, estimated by American military leaders to have numbered 145,000. This was correctly interpreted to mean that Washington had agreed to their continued presence in the South. As a result, Hanoi still had 145,000 soldiers in place after all American troops had left, while it had had only a few hundred in March 1965 when the first U. S. combat units arrived.

Thieu, who for propagandistic reasons, claimed that the number of North Vietnamese soldiers left in the South was 300,000 said any agreement that failed to guarantee the withdrawal of the North Vietnamese troops would not work which, coming from him, could only mean that it would not safeguard the survival of his regime.

After the Geneva Agreement of 1954, the Communists had to withdraw all their military forces, whether Northern or Southern, from the South. The fact that their much larger numbers were permitted after the 1973 cease-fire to remain in the South, must have led many Americans to the conclusion that even in purely military terms, the Communists were now in a better position to regain control of the entire country than they had been in 1954, and that therefore they would achieve their goal even if Thieu, with Nixon's consent, was to sabotage the political provisions of the Paris accord.

This was true in spite of the increase to over one million of the armed forces of the Saigon regime. Very few Americans believed that these demoralized forces, even with continued massive supplies of American weapons, could do what more than half a million American troops and the world's largest air force had failed to achieve. For these rightly skeptical Americans the Paris accord was what Stanley Hoffman called it after the collapse of the Saigon regime—"a screen behind which we got out, inevitably leaving Hanoi in place." The same conclusion was reached by Donald Kirk who, in *The New Leader* of December, 1972, wrote: "The prospect of ultimate failure for the United States is implied in the nature of the peace."

As to the U. S. government, the signing of the Paris cease-fire convinced many Americans that Washington was at last ready to do what a politically more sophisticated and morally more sensitive American leadership might have done after the Geneva Agreement of 1954: accept, at the risk of a Communist victory, a political solution for Vietnam.

Whether Washington in January, 1973 had really achieved this degree of political understanding will probably never be known, not even after Nixon's memoirs are published, since on the subject of Vietnam we can hardly expect him to be honest. Nor will we ever learn, either from Nixon or Kissinger, whether it was pressure or secret promises of renewed military help which got Thieu to accept an agreement he had refused to sign three months earlier. Some think that Nixon was convinced that the vastly increased and generously supplied South Vietnamese army would, if not actually defeat the army, certainly be able to prevent a Communist victory. Others believe that Nixon was secretly determined to resume American military intervention if necessary, and that assurances to that effect had prompted Thieu to sign the Paris accord. The fact that Nixon claimed South Vietnam would not have been lost if he had still been president in 1975 seems to confirm this, while the Christmas bombing may have convinced Thieu of Nixon's determination to prevent a Communist victory even if this required drastic and unpopular new military action.

It is quite certain, however, that Nixon knew the Saigon regime would sabotage the political provisions of the Paris accord, the implementation of which would have meant, if not a total Communist victory, at least the end of the Thieu regime. Nixon must have known that shortly before signing the Paris accord, Thieu threw into prison many non-Communist politicians suspected of favoring the agreed-upon political solution of the conflict. Furthermore, American policy after January, 1973 seems to confirm that Thieu's sabotage of the Paris accord had from the very beginning Nixon's approval and support. Since Washington did absolutely nothing to compel Thieu to implement the agreement it had made him sign, it is not at all surprising that the Paris cease-fire was regarded by most critics of our Vietnam policy as just another American fraud.

Finally, there are those who believe that a man of Nixon's intelligence must have realized that after the failure of American military intervention, victory by the Communists could no longer be prevented. To say so was of course impossible for Nixon, since it would have amounted to an admission that the policy the U. S. had pursued for over thirty years had been utterly mistaken.

Those who believe that Nixon knew at the end of 1972 that all was lost must be convinced that in order to get Thieu's signature to the Paris accords he had to deceive him with promises of renewed American military intervention. Whether he made these promises knowing that he could not keep them is mere speculation, as is the assumption that Nixon thought Saigon could still defeat the Communists. What is quite certain, however, is the conviction of the Communists that nothing could prevent their ultimate victory if, after the Paris cease-fire, the struggle for Vietnam became primarily a political contest.

III.
Thieu's Sabotage of the Paris Accord

A) THE POLITICAL PROVISIONS

Knowing that to grant even a minimum of the civil liberties provided for in the Paris accord would threaten the survival of his regime, President Thieu used his dictatorial powers with even less restraint after signing the cease-fire than before.

What was known about the terror which the Thieu regime applied to its critics and suspected political opponents before January 1973, was shocking enough to many Americans, particularly since its victims were largely non-Communists. A special branch of the national police arrested tens of thousands every year, and in roundups all over the country many of these were tortured and executed. *The New York Times* of December 22, 1972 reported a hunger strike by political prisoners in the Chi Hoa prison in Saigon, who had been picked up in the streets and jailed because they were "wrong-thinking" Catholics or students known to be disgusted with the Thieu regime. All of this got even worse between January, 1973 and April, 1975.

During my last visit to South Vietnam in April, 1973 I had ample opportunity to get confirmation of reports such as the one by Holmes Brown and Don Luce in *Hostages of War: Saigon's Political Prisoners*, which put their number at more than 200,000 (See my article "Thieu's Prisoners" in *The New York Review of Books*, of June 14, 1973). Much of what I wrote on this subject I had learned in dozens of interviews with knowledgeable senators, journalists, professors, lawyers and Catholic priests. The latter were at that time engaged in assembling all known facts about the number of prisoners and their mistreatment, in a clandestine document of 393 pages, in which Thieu's refusal to free them was called a shameless violation of the Paris accord (See *The Washington Post* of July 27, 1973).

This document proves not only that no political prisoners were released but that their number kept growing after January, 1973. Of this policy, the opposition deputy, Le Qui Chung, said, according to The Indochina Resource Center publication of November 1, 1974:

"The clampdown [on political opponents] is Thieu's last attempt to bring things under control. Now Thieu can rule only with blood. He has no other choice."

But no less significant than the arrest of more and more political dissidents was Thieu's policy of continued systematic erosion of civil liberties and constitutional procedures. Not only were the freedoms enumerated in the Paris accord not granted. More newspapers were closed, more people jailed for trying to hold meetings, and all opposition parties, no matter how meekly they expressed their views, were ruled illegal by presidential decree of May 12, 1973. All of this made the Thieu regime only worse than it had already been before the Paris accord, when Donald Kirk wrote in *The New Leader*, December, 1972: "Not since the dictator Ngo Dinh Diem has South Vietnam seen such wholesale arrests, crackdown on the press and other repressive measures."

Until the day his regime collapsed Thieu continued this policy of systematically violating the political provisions of the Paris accord. Among the people he had arrested during the last few weeks before his resignation were "three senators, one judge, four lawyers and two journalists, all with unimpeachable anti-Communist credentials" (Dong Duc Khoi).

Since neither Nixon nor, after him, Ford ever showed any concern for the "inexcusable cruelty" (Richard Holbrook) of Thieu's police or for Thieu's suppression of all traces of civil liberties, they must have been convinced that a "free" South Vietnam could survive only by becoming a more and more brutal dictatorship.

The Communists, sure that final victory would be theirs in a political contest, denounced Thieu's sabotage of the political provisions of the Paris accord. But much more upset than the Vietcong and Hanoi were the non-Communist spokesmen of the so-called Third Force. While the Communists could still hope for a military solution in their favor, no such prospect of achieving any of its goals existed for the Third Force. What its members were hoping for— freedom to organize and participate in an election and in a coalition government not totally dominated by the Communists—may have been an illusion. But for those who saw no other prospect of avoiding a Communist dictatorship, achievement of their goal was possible only if the political provisions of the Paris accord were implemented.

For this reason alone, the harshest critics of Thieu's sabotage of the Paris accord were spokesmen of the Third Force. One of them, General Duong Van Minh, who regarded the Third Force as "the key to peace" (*The New York Times* February 27, 1973), was among the first to point out, in an open letter to the Paris conference on February 22, 1973, that if the political provisions of the Paris accord are ignored by the Thieu regime, the "people's right to self-determination are empty words."

Stating again and again that he would not negotiate with the Communists and the Third Force, as provided for in the agreement he had signed, Thieu made it clear that he was as determined to sabotage the Paris accord as Diem had been to sabotage the Geneva Agreement. By his refusal to talk with the Vietcong leaders of the Provisional Revolutionary Government about creating the National Council of National Reconciliation and Concords, Thieu indirectly admitted that he was politically no less afraid of the Third Force than of the Communists. In a speech at Vinh Binh on April 14, 1974 Thieu called the Third Force—although it was largely composed of well-known Buddhists, Catholics, some labor leaders and even former military leaders, all known as anti-Communists—"a creation of the Communists," and its members traitors, against whom the government "will take appropriate measures." These measures were loss of jobs, imprisonment, and frequently also torture.

This brings to mind a remark made by former Special Assistant to the President, McGeorge Bundy, in his commencement address at the University of Texas (*The New York Times* June 29, 1975) during which he mentioned what he called the "unsung" South Vietnamese "who did persist on the side of liberty." "Unsung" by our government is right. But what Bundy did not say is that if anyone under the governments of Diem, Ky and Thieu insisted on demanding true liberty, he either had to become a refugee or go to jail.

One of the leading Catholics agitating for Thieu's resignation and for election on the basis of the Paris accord was the Reverend

Tranh Hu Thanh, whom Thieu had special reason to hate because of the priest's anti-corruption campaign. Thanh, although strongly in favor of continuing the struggle for a non-Communist South Vietnam, nevertheless advocated Communist participation in elections. (For more about Thanh's activity and political views, see *The New York Times* of October 19, 1974, and for a critical view of Thanh's position, see *Focal Point* of March 14, 1975.)

Another Catholic opponent of Thieu was Ngo Cong Duc, a relative of Vietnam's Archbishop Binh. Duc, who said Thieu "survives only on B-57s," had to flee from Saigon to escape being arrested.

Even a former military strongman, General Nguyen Khanh (an exile in Paris since 1965), who called Thieu "the quintessential symbol of corruption, ineptitude and despotism," now regarded the implementation of the political provisions of the Paris agreement "as the only way to achieve peace (*The New York Times* April 17, 1975).

More interesting still was what *The New York Times* reported on November 3, 1974 about the shift away from Thieu by Tran Quoc Buu, long South Vietnam's most prominent labor leader. Buu had for years supported the successive Saigon governments as firmly as George Meany had supported what Washington did in Vietnam. Now he too asked for implementation of the Paris accord and the establishment of democratic liberties. I was surprised when Meany, still firmly supporting Nixon on Vietnam, did not attack Buu for raising a demand which Thieu and probably also Nixon considered to favor the Communists.

Thoi-Bao-Ga of the Vietnamese Resources Center at Cambridge, Massachusetts, which could be called a Third Force publication of Vietnamese in the United States, wrote in its issue of February, 1974: "Democratic liberties must be restored by the Thieu regime so that political 'third force' people can come forward and operate freely." All the diverse elements of the Third Force, which represented perhaps a majority of the Vietnamese people, were in spite of their different political backgrounds unanimous, at least from early 1974 on, behind one demand: in order to bring peace to Vietnam, Thieu must resign.

This opposition to Thieu consisted of soldiers disgusted with their leaders, of disabled and embittered army veterans, of most students and intellectuals, of Buddhist and Catholic spokesmen still hoping to avoid total Communist control, and even of some patriotic and deeply worried civil servants. No less important was the hostile attitude toward the Thieu regime of the great mass of exploited peasants, who suffered more than any other part of the people from the continued heavy fighting all over the country.

Probably only a minority of the people opposed to the Thieu regime had become reconciled by 1974 to a Communist controlled united Vietnam, but a majority would very likely have preferred an end to the war through a political compromise. Such a solution would probably for a number of years have assured the survival of a "neutralist" South Vietnam under a so-called coalition government—something which at least until early April, 1975, when a military solution in favor of the Communist became a certainty, the Vietcong and Hanoi would still have gladly accepted, since they felt sure of ultimate victory through political compromise. As late as early April, 1975, General Duong Van Minh still believed that "the other side is looking for a political solution" (*The New York Times* April 4, 1975). But, as I wrote already in the summer of 1972, "there will be no political settlement of the war as long as the United States continues to maintain the present Saigon regime" (*A Dragon Defiant*, p. 117).

Frances FitzGerald, one of America's most penetrating critics of our Vietnam policy, was unfortunately right once more when she wrote four days after the signing of the Paris cease-fire: "This fragile truce is foredoomed" (*The Record*, Bergen County, New Jersey). It was foredoomed due to Thieu's sabotage of the Paris accord, which trapped the large non-Communist sections of the South Vietnamese people helplessly between their hated government and the Communists. If the Third Force had been allowed to become active, this would very likely have led the Communists to seek final victory on the slower road of political compromise, instead of becoming convinced in the spring of 1975 that their only choice was to pursue their goal with military means.

If it were true, as many Americans believe, that both sides were equally guilty regarding the military provisions of the Paris accord, the fact would remain that not the Communists, but the Saigon regime with U. S. support, broke the agreement by refusing to implement the political provisions. "The obstacle to an agreement after 1972 was not Hanoi but Saigon," wrote Anthony Lewis in *The New York Times* of April 24, 1975. Or, as Stanley Karnow said of the Paris cease-fire: "The main flaw in that deal was that the U. S. did nothing to compel Thieu to reach a political settlement with the Vietcong."

B) THE MILITARY PROVISIONS

I believe that the question as to which side was primarily responsible for the breakdown of the military provisions of the Paris cease-fire has been definitely settled by Maynard Parker's already-mentioned article in the January, 1975 issue of *Foreign Affairs*, whose editors not even George Meany would dare to accuse of having pro-Communist sympathies. What Parker says in his article "Vietnam: The War that Won't End" should be part of every attempt to explain what happened in Vietnam between January, 1973 and May 1, 1975, and why it happened.

Although a supporter of U. S. policy in Vietnam, Parker, who describes his purpose as simply "an attempt to portray the realities," says before dealing with his main subject:

I thought at the time, and still think, that President Nixon could have negotiated in 1969 a settlement very similar to the one he finally produced in 1973. Had peace come to Vietnam in 1969, it would have saved nearly 21,000 Americans and many, if not most, of the estimated 600,000 Vietnamese killed between 1969 and the end of 1972.

Parker, a keen political observer in many other respects, had strange illusions about Thieu's "political skill," which he claims "brought a period of unparalleled political stability to his country,"—he does not mention that this very fragile stability could be maintained only through unrestricted political terror. This, however, should not prevent any reader of Parker's article from seriously considering what he reports about the course of military events during the years 1973 and 1974.

After a lengthy and highly exaggerated description of the progress he thinks the United States made in Vietnam under President Thieu until the end of 1972, Parker states rather surprisingly: "In the 23 months since the cease-fire, it has become clear that all three American achievements in South Vietnam—political, economic and military—have begun to erode and are now in danger."

Apportioning blame for the breakdown of the truce is difficult continues Parker; nevertheless he feels obliged to say: "In retrospect, I am inclined to conclude that the South Vietnamese were the more guilty party, since their actions appear to demonstrate that they never really intended to implement the truce. On the other hand, according to diplomats in Saigon at the time, the Communists evidently did think there would be at least a period of peace and were unprepared for—and staggered by—the aggressiveness of the government's operations."

Describing what he calls "the first phase of the post-cease-fire," Parker continues: "Almost from the moment the agreement was signed, President Thieu, realizing that the balance of power was in his favor, took the offensive in an attempt to eradicate the Communist ink spots and confine the Communists to their sanctuaries."

Of the Communists' attitude at this time, Parker says: "The North Vietnamese have improved their base areas and modernized their army to an unprecedented extent, yet have not used their newly acquired muscles against the South Vietnamese."

Of the second phase, which began on January 4, 1974 with a speech by Thieu ordering his army "to hit [the Communists] in their base areas," and ended in May, 1974, Parker says that it "resulted in a marked increase in large scale ARVN [South Vietnamese army] operations."

It was only during the third phase that the Communists finally began to retaliate, by calling on their armed forces to regain the land and people lost since the cease-fire. According to Parker, the Communists started serious military action only on May 17, 1974, more

than fifteen months after Thieu had ordered his army first to eliminate the so-called ink spots held by the Communists, and later to
attack them in their base areas. What Parker called the "degree of
restraint shown by the North Vietnamese" seems to have astonished
him no less than it must have most of the readers of this revealing
article. But as Frances FitzGerald correctly wrote: "It was in the
interest of the P.R.G. [Provisional Revolutionary Government] and
Hanoi to prevent military violations of the cease fire.

Communist restraint is what must have prompted Noam
Chomsky to say in his well-known sarcastic manner that after Thieu
had "intensified political represssion and launched a series of military actions, the 'enemy' was so ungracious as to respond." And in
an article of the American-Vietnamese Third Force publication
Thoi-Bao-Ga, its editor said as early as October, 1973, that "ever
since the signing of the Paris Peace Agreements, the Thieu regime
has done everything possible to destroy the peace and provoke a full
scale resumption of the war." In the same issue, *Thoi-Boa-Ga* says:
"As the palace in Oslo is readied for the festivities [presentation of
the Nobel Peace Prize to Kissinger], Thieu continues to rain shells
on the Vietnamese countryside as fast as American factories can
produce them."

Other evidence of Saigon's aggressiveness came in February 10,
1973. A Wire Service Dispatch from South Vietnam said: "Since the
cease-fire became effective at 8 A.M. Saigon time January 28, the
South Vietnamese have reported 8,296 dead, of which more than
7,000 were said to be Communists and only 1,200 government
troops."

George Meany, ignoring the fact of Communist restraint in the
face of Saigon's military aggressiveness during 1973, and Saigon's
reports that the Communists were losing more than five times as
many men as the South Vietnamese, claimed that the Communists
had killed more South Vietnamese soldiers in 1973 than in any other
year (adding, without explanation, "except two").

What makes it hard for any supporters of U. S. policy in
Vietnam to refute Maynard Parker's evidence of Thieu's responsibility for the breakdown of the Paris cease-fire is the fact that Parker

himself remained a supporter of this policy to the end of the war. As
such he deplored the likelihood that Congress would substantially
cut aid to Saigon, predicting that this "would mean collapse of South
Vietnam and in all probability a takeover by the Communist forces."
Of the Saigon regime's moral decay as a major reason for its later
collapse, Parker said nothing.

Nevertheless, even with respect to the touchy subject of Communist troop infiltration from the North, he maintained a high degree of objectivity. He did not accept Theiu's claims that the
number of North Vietnamese troops in the South was 300,000 at the
time of the Paris accord, in contradiction to the official American
figure of 145,000. About additional infiltration Parker reports:

Although the North has sent approximately 145,000 men to the South since
the cease-fire, they have also ex-filtrated nearly 115,000 men back to North
Vietnam. The resulting net increase of 30,000 men basically accounts for
casualties and other routine replacements and indicates no new massive
buildup of men in the South, a buildup that would be a prerequisite for any
massive offensive.

Nothing precise is known about whether such a buildup, of
which there was no evidence when Parker wrote [his article] at the
end of 1974, actually took place during January and February,
1975—as American official propaganda and other advocates of increased aid for Thieu claimed. One of these was again George
Meany, who wrote in the *Trade Union News* of March-April, 1975:
"No sooner did it become clear that Congress intended to refuse
[such aid] than the North Vietnamese launched a full scale invasion
of the South." If there were, as Thieu insisted and Meany probably
believed, 300,000 North Vietnamese troops in the South at the
beginning of 1975, any military expert could confirm that Hanoi had
absolutely no need to infiltrate new ones in order to bring about,
together with the military units of the Vietcong, the collapse of the
South Vietnamese army—an army which at least after February
1975 gave increasing evidence of having lost the will to fight. As
Joseph Treaster reports in his already quoted, highly informative
article: when the South Vietnamese army went down in defeat, "it

had three times as many men as the North Vietnamese and Vietcong," which means that very few new North Vietnamese soldiers joined their approximately 150,000 comrades in the South at the beginning of 1975.

IV.
Why the Communists Favored a Political Solution

The Communists had favored a political solution ever since it appeared that it was a possible course. The first such occasion came about in March, 1946, six months after the French had started their Indochina war by attacking the Saigon Administration of the Provisional Executive Committee for the South. The March 6, 1946 agreement between France and the Hanoi government of Ho Chi Minh would have peacably returned within five years control of the entire country to the Communists. Only when France broke this agreement eight months later by extending her war of colonial reconquest to the North did the Communists, deprived of a sure political way of achieving their aim, begin to systematically organize armed resistance. After nearly eight years of fighting, the Communists, through the Geneva Agreement, were offered another opportunity to regain control of the entire country through peaceful means.

To say that the Communists were in principle opposed to the use of force in pursuing their political aims would of course be naive for someone like myself who has studied Communist theory and practice for nearly fifty years and rejected both from a democratic and socialist point of view. But it would be equally naive, not to say foolish, to believe the Communists preferred the use of force even when their cause could be won through essentially peaceful methods of political compromise.

In choosing the road of political compromise offered by the Geneva Agreement of 1954 the Communists hoped to bring all of Vietnam under their control through the elections of July 1956. This is well-known, but less well-known is how strictly and patiently the Hanoi regime abstained from the use of force to unify the country after 1954, and how long it took Ho Chi Minh to abandon the strategy of seeking victory through political compromise. This has only recently been proved more convincingly than ever before by the Chinese anti-Communist historian and political scientist King C. Chen, in the *Political Science Quarterly*, Summer, 1975. Chen shows that the Vietnamese Communists once again resorted to the use of force only in response to the force applied against them. This did not happen immediately after the U. S. and Ngo Dinh Diem had deprived them of certain victory through the July 1956 all-Vietnamese elections. It happened only three years later, after Diem had rejected all efforts by Hanoi to avoid civil war through political compromise. One last such effort was a plan by Hanoi's Premier Pham Van Dong "for the normalization of South and North relationships," proposed to Diem in December, 1958.

Already a year earlier, according to Philippe Devillers, as quoted by Chen, "responsible elements of the Communist Resistance in Indochina came to the conclusion that they had to act, whether Hanoi wanted it or not." But even these elements acted at the beginning only in self-defense, and not until two years after Diem had started his anti-Communist military campaign in mid-1955. (Diem himself claimed in May, 1956 that this campaign had in a period of ten months "entirely destroyed the predominant Communist influence of the previous nine years.") And it was not until January, 1959 that Hanoi approved in principle the resumption of the armed revolt the Communists in the South had started, a revolt now aiming at the overthrow of Diem, but still only in favor of a "coalition government."

This first Hanoi decision of January, 1959, on the resumption of the armed struggle in the South, Chen comments, "marked a departure from the party line of political struggle established after 1954," adding that "it was the growing military campaign of the Diem regime against the Communists with American support that compelled Hanoi to decide to revert to war." Diem's determination to rely on force for the survival of his regime was demonstrated by his claim that government forces had killed 440 Vietcong during 1959, and lost only 21 men, including officials killed or kidnapped. These figures also suggest how slowly the Communists mounted an armed resistance to Diem's military action against them.

Chen thinks that even as late as December, 1963, Hanoi was still determined "not to openly become involved in the war so as not to provoke the United States to retaliation." This, he believes, was one of the reasons why Hanoi had responded so eagerly to secret approaches which Diem and his brother Nhu made in the spring of 1963, obviously because Vietcong strength threatened to overthrow their hated regime.

Some details of this unsuccessful policy were revealed early in 1975 by the intermediary between Saigon and Hanoi, the Polish diplomat Mieczyslaw Maneli, whom Diem and Nhu, according to Chen, had asked "to approach the Hanoi government to explore the possibility for a peaceful solution of the conflict." During the summer of 1963, "Hanoi produced plans under which the North and South could gradually develop postal, economic, and cultural relations." In the article about his mission which Maneli wrote in *The New York Times* of January 27, 1975, entitled "Vietnam '63 and Now," he said "the North would not press for speedy reunification, but instead a coalition government would be set up in the South . . . Such a government could be headed by Diem." These plans also aimed at "neutralization" of South Vietnam, while North Vietnam, again according to Maneli, "would not become an aggressive outpost against other countries, and neither Soviet nor Chinese troops would under any conditions be allowed on Vietnamese soil."

Chen, who has no illusions about the true nature of Vietnamese Communism, thinks that Hanoi desired this kind of settlement for three reasons: economic difficulties in the North, fear of a deeper military conflict with the United States, and the strain of the Sino-Soviet rivalry in Vietnam. He also thinks that Hanoi "seemed to have believed that a neutralized South Vietnam would force the United States departure and would eventually work in favor of the Communist desire to take over the country."

The secret contacts between Saigon and Hanoi, first interrupted by the Diem regime's serious troubles with Buddhist resistance, ended with the overthrow of Diem on November 1, 1963. But even without Diem's overthrow, American opposition may well have prevented a peaceful solution to the conflict in 1964. In a telegram of January 1, 1964, to the new Chief of State General Duong Van Minh, President Johnson stated that "neutralization of South Vietnam would only be another name for a Communist takeover."

Apparently agreeing with Johnson, the junta of generals then in power in Saigon rejected new proposals made by Hanoi soon after the fall of Diem. (Chen believes that the United States may have endorsed the coup of the Saigon generals against Diem because they rejected the Saigon-Hanoi secret talks.) It was only after this rejection that the Communists, now definitely deprived of another chance to achieve victory through political compromise, once again reverted to the military strategy they had adopted in response to Diem's attempt to eliminate them from South Vietnam by force. They would have preferred a peaceful solution of the conflict even if it meant that they had to renounce total power for a long interim period.

When the Communists, just about nine years later, accepted with such obvious satisfaction first the October draft of 1972 and then the Paris cease-fire of January, 1973, it was again not because of an aversion to the use of force, but rather because of their conviction that the prospect of victory would improve if the struggle for Vietnam were to become at last a true political contest.

PART *Five*

The Inevitable Collapse

I.
Why Thieu Resigned Too Late

Up to a few weeks before the collapse of the Saigon regime on April 30, 1975, the Vietcong and Hanoi were still ready to accept a political settlement. The reason it did not come about was that Thieu, apparently convinced that in a political contest he was bound to lose to the Communists, did everything in his power, from the very day after signing the Paris accord, to perpetuate the war. Since he could hardly believe that the Communists could be defeated on the battlefield without direct American military support, his reasons for attacking enemy ink spots and base areas were not only to inflict heavy casualties. He was also trying to provoke serious cease-fire violations by the Communists, hoping that this would bring the United States back into the war.

However, once the Communists became convinced that Washington was not going to pressure Thieu into accepting a political solution to the conflict, and would probably not send American troops back to Vietnam, they were not at all reluctant to accept Thieu's military challenge. After they had begun to fight on all fronts, and from May 1974 on also undertaken attacks of their own, South Vietnamese and American propaganda spread the lie that the war continued because of Hanoi's systematic cease-fire violations.

Thieu continued his sabotage of the Paris agreement's political and military provisions up to the day of his resignation on April 21, 1975. This prompted Tom Wicker to write in *The New York Times* of March 28, 1975: "It would be far better to twist Mr. Thieu's arm, as Mr. Kissinger did not hesitate to twist at the time of the Paris accords in 1973, to enter into peace negotiations with Hanoi, while something is left to negotiate."

Although this somewhat contradicts Thieu's complaint to Oriana Fallaci on December 30, 1972, when he found it "disgusting" that America's concern for the 500 captured pilots in Hanoi made it possible for the North Vietnamese "to impose political conditions on us" *(The New Republic,* January 20, 1973), it does not exclude Kissinger's having spoken the truth when he said in April, 1975 that Thieu, before signing the cease-fire agreement, had been promised "vigorous action" if the North Vietnamese violated the truce on a large scale *(The New York Times*, April 22, 1975). Formal confirmation of any such promise was still lacking when the *Times* wrote on the same day: "Enough is known now, however, to indicate that President Thieu was given to believe that he could count on Washington's military and political support for his government to an extent far beyond the written agreement signed in Paris."

It is hard to know what to believe of statements by people like Thieu and our own leaders whose political predicament after January 1973 made it virtually impossible for them to be truthful. But it is clear today that Thieu was speaking the truth when he said that Nixon had promised to prevent his defeat by the Communists and that Nixon had really given a "solid pledge" to that effect.

William Buckley, who permits his intelligence to be constantly nullified by primitive prejudices, confirmed Nixon's alleged "solid pledge" by writing that Congress denied President Thieu the American war materiel "we had promised South Vietnam in the event of a violation of the Paris accord." Like Thieu himself, who in his resignation speech complained about "flagging American military support," Buckley ignored the fact that South Vietnam, as Dennis Trout reported in *Harper's* Magazine of July, 1975 had, since the signing of the Paris treaty, been receiving "roughly six times as much [military aid] as his opponents in Hanoi."

I hope it will soon be recognized as ridiculous to say that after the U.S. had spent 160 billion dollars, Congress was failing to honor a commitment by refusing a further 700 million, for a cause which most Americans certainly had begun to regard as lost. Nevertheless, Ford and Kissinger kept blaming Congress for the "loss" of South Vietnam, long after most U.S. allies had become convinced that we failed in Vietnam not, as Hans Horganthau put it, because of our "reluctance to meet commitments but because of the irremediable weakness of the regime to whose survival we were committed."

Congress wisely ignored a warning by Kissinger, who at the end of March, 1975 said that "to destroy an ally by withholding aid from it would have a 'cataclysmic' . . . impact on the United States' position in the world." This idea, which after the collapse of the Saigon regime was also taken up by President Ford and many other bewildered defenders of Thieu's South Vietnam, implied that Congress had seriously damaged American national interests by at last taking a stand that put an end to our senseless military involvement in Vietnam. The truth is, as I will show later on, that by taking this stand, Congress had in the opinion of most U.S. allies improved its political and military position in the world.

It is possible that, at least up to the beginning of April 1975, Ford could have ended the war by forcing Thieu either to resign or to accept immediate negotiations aiming at a compromise. Even as late as April 2, the Paris delegate of the Provisional Revolutionary Government stated that the Communists still favored a political solution. This, of course, may have been propaganda designed to strengthen the opposition of Third Force circles to Thieu.

Some American observers, such as Robert Shaplen, believe that the Communists had decided before the end of March to seek victory on the battlefield. According to other reports, however, they urged French Ambassador Jean-Marie Merillon to arrange political negotiations even as their troops were already approaching Saigon.

Robert Shaplen thinks that "the two weeks lost before Thieu finally resigned may have been the last chance to avoid the abrupt total American withdrawal and allow the South Vietnamese a more decent surrender." This chance no longer existed when Thieu resigned on April 21, as James Wechsler pointed out in *The New York Post* of April 22 by quoting a State Department official: "Saigon is just hanging there ripe for the picking. I can't see why [the Communists] would wait and let the fruit fall when they can just reach for it now."

Robert Shaplen, still in Saigon at that time, believed that by April 22 the Communists ran out of patience, and were no longer interested in a tri-partite government under the terms of the Paris agreement. What they wanted now was a new Saigon regime willing to accept unconditional surrender. Implying that a more vigorous Third Force action might perhaps have led to a tri-partite government (which of course required Thieu's resignation), Shaplen puts part of the blame on the "quarrelsome [anti-Communist] Southern leaders who moved far too late and far too slow to establish a new government."

Whether better cooperation and more energetic action among the non-Communist opponents of Thieu could have achieved this goal, no one can now be sure. What is certain, however, is the conclusion drawn by Frances FitzGerald in her first comment (May 3, 1975) about the end of the Indochina war: Thieu "waited until it no longer mattered to resign."

Although for a long time convinced, as were most of my socialist and liberal friends, that in the end Hanoi and the Vietcong were certain to achieve victory, I was nevertheless surprised by the speed with which military events between March 10 and early April, 1975 moved toward the inevitable collapse of the Saigon regime.

After the Paris accord I was again involved in efforts to bring about, through pressure by Washington on Thieu, an end to the war through political compromise. I responded immediately when a U.S. Senator asked me in April, 1975 to put on paper my reasons for believing that a peaceful solution, if still possible, could come about only through an immediate decision by President Ford. The Senator's specific request was that I draft a letter he would then address to the President, hoping that my arguments would persuade

Mr. Ford to do what I proposed as an urgent step on his part: "To side with the non-Communist opponents of Thieu by publicly supporting their demand that Thieu resign."

I know that this letter of eight typewritten pages, which I wrote during the night of April 15 to 16, was taken to the Senator on the following day. What I do not know is whether it ever reached the President, and whether, if he read it at all, it had anything to do with what happened only a few days later. "After procrastinating for weeks," Robert Shaplen wrote, "[Ambassador] Graham A. Martin, with the help of French Ambassador Jean Marie Merillon, persuaded President Nguyen Van Thieu to resign."

But when the news of Thieu's resignation reached me, I was already convinced that the letter I had drafted five days before Thieu resigned should have been written at least four weeks earlier. Not that I think it had anything to do with Thieu's belated decision, nor do I believe that there would have been much chance of his taking this step in the middle of March. Nor is it certain that Thieu's removal four weeks earlier would have spared the Vietnamese people another six weeks of war, nor that it would have decidedly altered the final outcome. But it might at least have allowed the South Vietnamese non-Communist leaders—to quote Shaplen again—"a more decent surrender."

More time and a chance for a decent negotiated surrender was again lost by the appointment (before General Duong Van Minh) of Tran Van Huong as successor to Thieu, since Huong "completely disregarded the reality of the situation" (Shaplen) and instead of seeking immediate contact with the Vietcong, insisted that the war continue. This, of course, convinced the Communists that they had been right when they had decided, probably two or three weeks before Thieu's resignation, that they had no choice but to insist on the military decision which would soon make them masters of the whole country.

That a chance for a negotiated settlement of the conflict no longer existed after the end of March, 1975 was also the opinion of Ton That Tien, a friend since 1954 and a political adviser of General Duong Van Minh, one of the most prominent non-Communist op-

ponents of Thieu. Of Tien's pessimistic outlook I had already become aware when I saw him last in Saigon in early April, 1973.
According to *The New York Times* of April 1, 1975, Tien told an
American correspondent that the Communists had won the war,
adding: "Why should they be interested in a coalition and negotiations now"? Tien apparently no longer believed what the Communists had said in a broadcast on March 31: that they were still
ready to hold talks with a Saigon government committed to "peace,
independence, democracy, national concord and the strict applica-
tion of the Paris Agreement."

Unfortunately Ton That Tien was right when he had told me, in
April, 1973: unless Washington stops supporting Thieu, South
Vietnam will be Communist within two years. When Thieu finally
resigned—whether or not as a result of American pressure—it was
too late for any other solution.

II.
Collapse of an Army and Regime

The swift and dramatic collapse of the South Vietnamese army and
the Saigon regime was not the result of an overwhelming attack by
superior military forces. It came about because of the degree of
moral disintegration the South Vietnamese army had reached in
1975. This in turn reflected the degree of moral and political decay
to which South Vietnamese society had sunk after years of increasing political terror, mass misery and corruption. Moral disintegration alone can explain why an army three times the size and possess-
ing more than five times the equipment of the enemy could be as
rapidly defeated as the ARVN was between March 10 and April 30,
1975. Even CIA reports, which Ambassador Martin consistently
refused to take seriously, were "detailing the almost total collapse of
the South Vietnamese Army's military capacity and morale" (Shaplen).

When this army's low morale led to the final collapse—partly
due to the desertion of its corrupt leaders—large groups of soldiers
turned into hordes of plunderers, murderers and rapists, more

dangerous for the great mass of refugees, as well as for the populations of many towns, than the advancing Vietcong and North Vietnamese soldiers. It was, as Ronald Steel put it: "The collapse of a regime rotted from within, with raping and pillaging by the soldiers of a demoralized army, with the panicked surge of a people fleeing war." At many places, local members of the Saigon militia stopped these people and asked for bribes to let them proceed.

From the many reports about these horrors toward the end of the war I shall concentrate on what became known about the suffering inflicted on the people of Danang before the arrival of the Communist troops.

There, the army, after most of its officers had fled by air, completely fell apart, even while the enemy was still far away. Thousands of soldiers, many of them in stolen civilian clothes, not only looted all over town, sacking hospitals and stealing drugs: they also shot civilians, including children. The streets of Danang were littered with bodies.

Dennis Trout, in *Harper's Magazine* of July 1975, gives shocking details of these events. One can understand that embittered soldiers "wrenched open the doors of government rice storehouses, grabbing at the food that indifferent superiors often did not deliver to their families or to them in the field." But they also "turned to the women who often had men other than soldiers, but now were too shocked to resist the rough hands that pulled them into the narrow alleys of Danang and held them down while others mounted."

Those who succeeded in getting on a boat to flee Danang were not safe either. "The soldiers' rampage continued, but there was no escape for the victims who were robbed and raped within the confines of the boats" (Trout). Some civilians were killed when they stood in the way of soldiers fighting to get on an overcrowded boat, and many were also thrown overboard.

In their attempt to get out of Danang as quickly as possible, some soldiers kept shooting their way onto planes, killing, as if in revenge, airforce officers who demanded huge bribes from soldiers for rides on their planes (Fox Butterfield, New York Times May 28, 1975). South Vietnamese troops, having been told that the U.S. had abandoned them after luring them into the war, even fired on American aircraft, which caused some Americans in Saigon to fear that they too might be attacked by the South Vietnamese army.

Nothing shows more convincingly the disintegration of the Saigon armed forces than the nightmarish events at Danang thirty-six hours before the arrival of the Communist troops. On March 26, the Saigon troops, numbering 50,000, were still an organized military force, with a supply of arms sufficient for a six months' siege. Thirty-six hours later, the Saigon army had disintegrated into hordes of thieves, murderers and rapists. Danang fell to the Communists without a single shot having been fired by its defenders, except on some of the city's civilians.

This stage of disintegration had not yet been reached on March 10, when the Communist-led local Montagnard troops started to attack the highland city of Ban Me Thuot. The city fell after only four days of fighting, but its fall led to Saigon's decision to withdraw all its troops from the three highland provinces of Darlac, Pleiku and Kontum. They were abandoned as indefensible on March 17, 1975.

If the defense of Ban Me Thuot showed that the South Vietnamese army was still able to offer some resistance, it nevertheless proved that its heart was not longer in it. Ban Me Thuot also proved that the Communists could win some battles even without the direct participation of the North Vietnamese army. According to an escaped Catholic priest, no Hanoi troops were involved in the battle for Ban Me Thuot. He reported also that many of the government troops, after being defeated by the local Montagnards, remained in town with them (*Washington Post*, March 15, 1975).

On March 19 Quang Tri City fell to the Communists; on March 25 the Provisional Revolutionary Government established control over Hué, which had been completely isolated since March 23. There, the Communists met no more resistance than they met four days later at Danang.

This series of Communist victories continued through April. Fox Butterfield reported in *The New York Times* of April 10 that at the beginning of April Saigon had lost half of its 1.1 million troops.

Although the Communists, between March 29 and April 2 had

taken all of South Vietnam down the coast from Danang to Phan Thiet 100 miles east of Saigon, President Ford, ignoring the fact that the Saigon troops fled faster than the Communists were able to follow, said on April 3 that he "does not anticipate the fall of South Vietnam."

He probably lost his illusions—temporarily strengthened by evidence at Xuan Loc that some units of the Saigon army were still willing to fight—only by April 30, when the fall of Saigon completed the collapse of the South Vietnamese army. On this regime, which Washington had adopted in 1954 and had now definitely "lost," the United States had wasted money for nearly twenty-one years and lives for more than ten. These efforts failed because it was impossible, as *The New York Times* said in an editorial of May 6, 1975 to save "a regime that never took root."

Further evidence that the rapid and complete collapse of the Saigon regime was largely due to its loss of even the shaky popular support it might have enjoyed, was the easy way in which the Communists were able to establish political control over the towns and provinces abandoned by the South Vietnamese army. They had no trouble at all gaining the co-operation of many non-Communists leaders of the Third Force, especially Buddhists, who joined the People's Revolutionary Committee in Hué and Danang only a few days after the Communists occupied these cities. Some of these leaders also issued appeals to their followers to remain and co-operate with the new administration.

One of the reasons for this attitude was the conviction of many leaders of the Third Force that most South Vietnamese welcomed the victory of the Communists, even if only because they had become convinced by mid-April that there was no other way to end the war. In Danang, for instance, the population, after thirty-six hours of mistreatment by South Vietnamese soldiers, had only one wish: "that the Vietcong would arrive as quickly as possible to restore order, any order" (*The New Republic*, May 17, 1975). When the first Vietcong troops arrived, the looting and shooting suddenly stopped. In every city taken over by the Communists, order was quickly established, shops were reopened and public services made again available for the needy. After having been robbed of much of their goods, Danang's shopowners were happy to learn that Vietcong soldiers entered their shop not to steal but to buy. The entire population of Danang was grateful when the Communist soldiers, only a few days after their arrival, were ordered to remove the 250 tons of garbage that had been littering the city for months.

The Communists no doubt also gained new popular support by releasing the more than 200,000 persons kept in prison for political reasons by the Thieu regime. In Ban Me Thuot, for instance, they let the prisoners' families open the prisons to free them. After April 30, the Communists also abolished Thieu's infamous "tiger cages," where numerous prisoners had become cripples. These and similar measures were taken not so much for humanitarian as for obvious political reasons. The Communists, themselves never averse to imprisoning or killing people they considered dangerous political enemies, knew better than their American and other critics that terror is to be used only when necessary to gain and maintain power. Unlike the Thieu regime, which could probably not have lasted more than a month without applying terror to its enemies, the Communists, who had "gone out of their way to emphasize to their cadres their aim of reconciliation with the South" (Shaplen), had absolutely no need for tiger cages or other methods of terrorizing the people of South Vietnam.

According to the Indochina Resources Center in Washington, the firepower ratio in favor of the South Vietnamese army was 7-1, and even conservative estimates put the value of the American military equipment picked up by the Communists during March and April, 1975—including 300 aircraft—at one billion dollars, more than twice the amount Hanoi had received from China and Russia in two years. In view of this fact and considering that he had gone along with Thieu's sabotage of the Paris accord, Kissinger must have known that he was again trying to deceive the American people when he stated, according to *The New Yorker* of May 5, 1975: "We shall never forget who supplied the arms which North Vietnam used to make a mockery of its signature on the Paris accord."

III.
"Bloodbath" and Refugees

In an attempt to frighten Congress into voting further funds for the Saigon regime, Vice President Nelson Rockefeller made what may well be the most irresponsible statement of his entire political career. He said if "the Communists take over and there are a million people killed, we know where the responsibility will lie."

Although some Americans in Saigon believed, as Robert Shaplen reported, "that as many as a hundred thousand people could be killed," at least one U. S. official in Saigon admitted to a French newspaper correspondent: "Well, honestly, we are making a lot of this issue because it can affect ongoing deliberations [in Congress] of the aid program."

After the blood the U.S. had caused to be spilled in Vietnam, our leaders should have realized that "we are the last who should speak of blood baths" (Stanley Hoffman).

Less surprising is that the Saigon leadership tried to exploit this theme, in a campaign consisting of nothing but inventions and lies. Two West-German correspondents in Saigon, Klaus Liedke and Hans Bollinger, dealt at great length with this subject in an article in the West-German magazine *Stern* of June 5, 1975. Confirming Dennis Trout's writing that "blood bath stories were dredged up and replanted in the anxious imaginations of overworked Saigon reporters," Liedke and Bollinger detailed these stories. Saigon propaganda claimed that the Communists slaughtered the children of Vietnamese mothers and American fathers, gathered people in the cities for mass-execution, raped Catholic nuns and killed Buddhist monks by burning them.

In order to find out whether any of these stories were true, these two reporters arranged, not without difficulty, to be taken by boat, on April 27, 1975, from Vungtau on the coast south-east of Saigon to Phan Thiet, which had been in Communists hands since April 2. They were well received and well treated by the local Vietcong army and administration, but in spite of constant urgings, not allowed to return to Saigon until May 8.

At Phan Thiet, Liedke and Bollinger were unable to find confirmation for any kind of Communist atrocities. During their stay they met an American and a Japanese who had been working for the Mennonites and had walked from Danang to Phan Thiet, which had taken them two weeks. "In their talks with peasants and inhabitants of the cities," Liedke and Bollinger wrote, "they did not hear of a single case of acts of revenge by the Communists (they called them rebels) against civilians or government soldiers."

Among the many others who looked for but could not find evidence of Communist atrocities was George Esper, who, in a report from Saigon (*The New York Times* May 9, 1975) stated simply, a week after the Communists had taken Saigon: "I saw no blood bath." Esper also was told by a former South Vietnamese army captain that the North Vietnamese, when they caught up with fleeing South Vietnamese soldiers, did not shoot at them but fired into the air. "If they had tried to kill them," the captain said, "they could have killed everybody." After the fall of Quang Tri on March 19, 1975, the Vietcong forces, instead of killing their defeated enemies, helped Saigon soldiers to evacuate the town.

Indeed, the only blood bath of which there is so far any evidence in Vietnam was the massacre of civilians by the disintergrating South Vietnamese army.

American and South Vietnamese propaganda, referring to the millions of refugees the long war had produced in Vietnam, took this as proof that it was fear of Communist atrocities which made people flee, especially during March and April, 1975, those parts of the country about to be overrun by the Vietcong and the North Vietnamese. But what Anthony Lewis wrote about the more than 800,000 people who became refugess during 1973 remained true also in 1975. They "fled their homes to escape war" (*The New York Times* February 7, 1974). *Indochina Focal Point* of April 5-25, 1975, for instance, quoted a woman interviewed by a New York Times reporter, as saying that it was better for people to go to the Saigon side where they would not be bombed since the Communists had no airplanes. Many members of her family and friends, she explained, had stayed in Quang Tri after it fell to the Communists in 1972.

There was bombing and shelling by the Saigon forces all the time, and many were killed. Of those who stayed at Ban Me Thuot when the town fell to the Communists (of 170,000, 150,000 remained) many must have regretted their decision when Saigon planes struck the town twice on March 20, killing and wounding four hundred people. A day before this attack, the entire region, including Pleiku and Kontum, had been declared free fire zones for the Saigon airforce.

Most of the refugees, *The New York Times* reported on March 26, 1975, "appear to be fleeing in panic rather than for political reasons." This was of course not true of every one of these refugees, since there were many who believed, rightly or wrongly, that they would be punished by the Communists. About these people at Danang, for instance, Malcolm Browne reported in *The New York Times* of March 28: "Those who fear the Communists most were at the airport. Waiting at the field were the families of military officers and policemen, businessmen and the more prosperous shopkeepers. There were also Roman Catholics from what is now North Vietnam . . ." Brown however concluded that "most of the rest of the people of Danang . . . seemed content to stay."

Most peasants too knew that any area falling under Vietcong control was likely to suffer artillery fire and bombing by the Saigon army and airforce. When they fled, they were running from the war, not as the American public was told, "voting with their feet." They were often joined, especially after March, 1975, by South Vietnamese soldiers who, by throwing away their arms and uniforms, made themselves also refugees.

Many who became refugees in March and April, 1975, Fox Butterfield wrote in *The New York Times* of March 28, "were more afraid of the [Saigon] rangers than they were of the Vietcong."

No American paper I know of ever seems to have mentioned what well-informed Europeans knew: that some South Vietnamese also fled from Saigon-occupied into Communist-held territory. Nor did I read in any American paper that the old Queen Mother (the mother of Vietnam's last "emperor" Bao Dai) refused to leave her palace at Hue before the Communists took the city.

One of the reasons why so many people stayed and others quickly returned to their homes in Communist-occupied territory was no doubt the attitude of the Roman Catholic church, entirely different from what it had been in 1954, when over half a million Catholics left the Communist North. What a prominent Catholic priest, reflecting on the possibility that Saigon might fall to the Communists, told me in April, 1973, another church leader expressed with the same two words to the French journalist and historian Jean Lacouture in April, 1974: "We remain" (*New York Review of Books* May 1, 1975). Another Catholic, Bishop Pham Ngoc Chi, whom I knew well after he had fled in 1954 from the North to Saigon, also decided to stay, even before the Roman Catholic Archbishop of Saigon, Nguyen Van Binh, called upon the Catholics to remain in areas newly occupied by the Communists. Having received word from the Vatican "to lie low and make whatever accommodations with the Communists they can" (Shaplen), all Catholic bishops remained at their posts during the weeks of the Communist advance, and so far not one has left since the fall of Saigon.

This, incidentally, is true also of most of my South Vietnamese political friends, all of them former anti-Communists opponents of Thieu. As far as I know, not a single one has been arrested or in any way mistreated by the Communists. Like the former presidential candidate Truong Dinh Dzu, who was thrown into jail by Thieu after he had, on a peace platform, gained the highest number of votes among the ten civilian candidates who opposed Thieu in the elections of September, 1967, they all have remained unmolested.

Even former officers and government officials were not arrested but had only to turn themselves in and agree to be "re-educated," which in the case of less important former Saigon official and low-grade military leaders meant that they were kept and lectured to for a few days. Reports from Saigon in October 1975 indicated that former high officials and even generals who have been kept in re-education localities, are being permitted to return to their homes and families. (For a more detailed report on "re-education," see *Le Monde diplomatique*, September, 1975.)

The New York Times of May 5, 1975 reported that General Duong Van Minh, for a few days the Saigon regime's last president, and eighteen former high government officials, temporarily detained after April 30, had been freed. Shortly afterwards, General Minh was even permitted to fly to Hanoi to visit his brother, Duong Van Nhat.

Huynh Tan Phat, the Prime Minister of the Provisional Revolutionary Government (a 62-year-old former Saigon architect) told the pro-Communist Australian journalist Wilfred Burchett at Saigon (now Ho Chi Minh City) early in October the reasons why the new masters of South Vietnam considered it advisable to abstain from using what would probably have been unnecessary terror. Quoted by Burchett in the pro-Chinese Communist American weekly *Guardian* of October 22, 1975, this is what Huynh Tan Phat wants the world to think determined the victorious Communists' attitude toward the South Vietnamese people:

We could not just rely on our military superiority. We had to take into account the people's state of mind. More bloodshed was the last thing they wanted. Their deepest desire was for peace. The use of force against hostile elements would only have created more tensions and served no useful purpose. If we had used force we would not have been able to rally the people to our side. Our fundamental policy was that of peace and national concord. That is why we decided on a step-by-step approach in dealing with the enemy, causing division in their ranks, isolating the most reactionary elements.

All reports from Saigon since April 30 seem to confirm that the Communists really stuck to this highly sophisticated policy toward the people and their political enemies in the South. Although Robert Shaplen expressed a fear (May 19, 1975) that some killings might occur, "especially at the village level where animosities are deepest," *The New York Times*, as late as July 14, published a U.P.I. report from Saigon which said that "there has apparently been little retaliation on any level and virtually none against former members of the Thieu government or army."

Nevertheless, it would be naive to expect Vice President Rockefeller to admit that he was mistaken when he predicted that a million people would be killed, or to express satisfaction that nothing like that happened when the Communists conquered South Vietnam.

PART *Six*

Consequences and Lessons

I.
Effect on Allies and Enemies

Another argument with which, as with the prediction of a horrible bloodbath after a Communist victory, the Administration tried to pressure Congress into voting for additional military aid to Saigon, dealt with the effect the "loss" of South Vietnam would have on both America's allies and its enemies.

Nixon had tried to frighten the American people and weaken its growing opposition to the war by saying in his first major presidential address on Vietnam (November 3, 1969): "A nation cannot remain great if it betrays its allies and lets down its friends. Our defeat and humiliation in South Vietnam without question would promote recklessness in the councils of those great powers who have not yet abandoned their goals of world conquest."

Repeated statements by the Ford Administration during the critical weeks before the fall of Saigon, claiming that our failure in Vietnam would drastically reduce America's influence everywhere else in the world, were apparently no longer made with the sole purpose of putting pressure on Congress. When Kissinger, on March 25, 1975, said that to destroy an ally by withholding aid would have a "cataclysmic" impact on the United State's position in the world, I was probably not the only one among the many opposed to more aid for Thieu who had the impression that Kissinger was really afraid this would happen.

This fear was also expressed by some non-governmental supporters of our Vietnam policy, both before and after we had "lost" South Vietnam. One of these, apparently more obsessed by it than Ford and Kissinger themselves, was Earl C. Ravenal, Adjunct Professor at Johns Hopkins School of Advanced International Studies and Fellow of the Washington Center for Foreign Policy Research. Ravenal who, even after the fall of Saigon, still thinks that the "hawks" had always been closer to the truth than the "doves," wrote in his long article "Consequences of the End Game in Vietnam" in the July, 1975 issue of *Foreign Affairs:* "We cannot abandon friends in one part of the world without jeopardizing the security of friends everywhere." What Ravenal calls the failure of Congress to provide enough assistance and our willingness to abandon the field when we think we have done enough prompted him to say that "President Thieu's parting complaint, though querulous and ungrateful, was, in this particular sense, quite accurate"—meaning that the U. S. had betrayed South Vietnam. The reliability of American response Ravenal calls the first casualty of Vietnam, and he says that other potential allies "ought to be more wary about inviting the United States to participate in their troubles" (which indeed they should, although for reasons which this scholar will grasp only if he conducts his future foreign policy research with a more open mind).

Fear that failure in Vietnam might damage America's position in the world was at one time expressed even by *The New York Times*, whose merits in correcting the American people's misconceptions about Vietnam I hope will never be forgotten. On August 14, 1961, *The New York Times* wrote: "If the U. S. cannot win or will not save South Vietnam from Communist assault, no Asian nation can ever again feel safe in putting its faith in the U. S." But on May 4, 1975, the same paper, after nearly ten years of gradually increasing opposition to the war, stated: "Contrary to the view reiterated by Defense Secretary Schlessinger last week, disengagement from a civil war in which the United States should never have become engaged need not shake this country's position in the world."

CONSEQUENCES AND LESSONS

Most of our best writers on foreign policy have by now rejected what Hans Morgenthau called the idea of a declining and unreliable America, which our leaders "for psychological and political reasons of their own have propagated." It is simply not true that America has become weaker since April 30, 1975, and that our allies no longer trust us.

I have long been convinced that the opposite was likely to happen when we once got out of Vietnam. This view, strengthened with an additional argument, was well expressed by James Reston, who, with reference to the fact that the American people was deeply divided by the Vietnamese war, wrote in *The New York Times* of May 14, 1975: "The truth is that a united America out of Southeast Asia is stronger and more reliable than a divided America fighting for dubious goals around Saigon."

Hans Morgenthau is now convinced that "our friends and allies [are] neither surprised nor disheartened by the collapse of American policy in Indochina," adding that he has "not seen in any serious European or Israeli publication a reference to a decline of America's power, to lack of trust in America's commitments, or to the domino theory as a valid analysis of world politics."

"If anything," James Chace wrote in the same issue of *The New Republic*, "most Europeans, long weary of America's distraction from traditional geopolitical areas of interest, are relieved that U. S. power and political will can now be once again put into proper balance."

To strengthen this particular point, Chace praised former West German Chancellor Willy Brandt for, shortly before the fall of Saigon, dismissing "as groundless fears that a refusal by the United States to provide [more] military aid for Indochina would provoke Europeans to question America's commitments to Western Europe."

To quote Morgenthau again: "What the outside world doubts is neither America's power nor reliability, but the capacity of its leaders to lead, and more particularly, to lead wisely."

Not only our European allies but Japan too, as Keyes Beach wrote in *Saturday Review* of August 13, 1975, preferred the United States out of Vietnam rather than in it. After stating that most

Japanese could never understand what we were doing in Vietnam anyway, Beach, in his article "Japan—the Ultimate Domino?" gives the following description of how one prominent Tokyo political scientist challenged the view that America was no longer to be trusted because it had "betrayed" the old Saigon regime. "What, he asked tartly, did the critics want the United States to do? Become militarily involved in Vietnam a second time? Personally, he added, he had gained, rather than lost, trust in the United States because of its refusal to make the same mistake twice."

Some have taken as proof of a sharp decline of America's position, at least in Asia, the fact that Thailand and the Philippines began to seek, after the fall of Saigon, normal diplomatic relations with The People's Republic of China. The truth is that first steps toward this end were taken by these two countries at least three years before the collapse of the Saigon regime, no doubt encouraged by Kissinger's and Nixon's visits to Peking.

As if motivated by a desire to balance what the cold warrior Ravenal had written for it, *Foreign Affairs* published in the same issue an article by Alistair Buchan, who argued that neither the European NATO countries nor Japan felt their security had been improved by American persistance in trying to save an anti-Communist South Vietnam.

As far as I am concerned, Vietnam has damaged the United States abroad only by destroying the claim that in coming to the aid of an anti-Communist regime, America was acting in defense of freedom. Our military intervention in Indochina proved that the U. S., in order to defend what it considered (in this case mistakenly) its own national interests, was ready to maintain the most brutal dictatorship, even if this required going to war.

This brings to mind a remark Kissinger made in a speech in Birmingham, Alabama, on August 14, 1975: "This Administration shall never forget the moral difference between freedom and tyranny" (*The New York Times* August 15, 1975). One might be tempted to say that Kissinger cannot forget this difference because he does not yet seem to know it. His defense over many years of what the U. S. did in Vietnam proves that for him—and, unfortunately, for too many other American political leaders—an anti-democratic regime is tyrannical only if it is Communist. If a country's dictatorship is anti-Communist, no matter how tyrannical, it is part of the "free world." In spite of Thieu's truly tyrannical regime, South Vietnam thus remained to them one of the countries which, as President Ford said in a press conference on June 9, 1975, believe in freedom as we do.

Not even George Orwell could have foreseen that the president of the largest democratic country in the world would, long before 1984, explain that the purpose of aid to tyrannical regimes like that of Saigon's Thieu was to enable them "to protect the freedom of their citizens."

The reader may have noticed that I never called the South Vietnamese dictatorships from Diem to Thieu fascist. There is a good historical reason for this: no matter how totalitarian some of the dictatorships are which the U. S. still supports around the world, they should be called fascist only if, in gaining power and at least temporarily maintaining it they can rely on—in addition to political terror—some organized mass support, something possessed by Mussolini, Hitler, and even Franco, but not by any of the South Vietnamese regimes.

II.
Lessons, Right and Wrong

There can be no doubt that the end of the war was greeted with a feeling of great relief all over the United States. But no matter how glad most Americans were, other feelings, aroused during the long years of war, persisted. When Robert Lowell wrote "I am glad the war is finished, despite the poison it leaves behind," he must have had in mind the widespread fear of a long and bitter national debate about this tragic episode in the history of the United States. Popular anger over the brutality and disgraceful failure of U. S. intervention, it was thought, might lead old critics to intensify and new ones to support their attacks against the policies five administrations had pursued in Indochina.

Aware of the immense disadvantage at which they would find themselves in such a debate, our responsible leaders, especially President Ford, kept insisting that the American people wants to forget Vietnam, or as Kissinger put it authoritatively: "The Vietnam debate has run its course."

One of the many authors unwilling to stop discussing Vietnam is Mary McCarthy, who wrote of our leaders' wish to forget all about Vietnam: "That, obviously, is the opposite of learning a lesson."

Among those who insist that the debate continue are many longtime opponents of the war, who had, years ago, learned most of the lessons which our failure in Vietnam might now teach the American people. This is especially true for critics who had foreseen how the war would end. One of these, Richard Holbrooke, wrote right after the fall of Saigon: "For at least eight years it seemed reasonable to me to assume that sooner or later, no matter what we did in Vietnam, things would end badly for us." Another one, Donald Kirk, wrote in *The New Leader* of December 25, 1972: "In the end, unless the scenario holds some surprises now impossible to see, North Vietnam will win it all."

Apparently assuming that most people in the U. S. must have come to realize during the last year or two before the end what Holbrooke had foreseen eight years earlier, Chester Cooper remarked that "Americans have a right to be saddened, but not surprised by what has happened."

Being saddened is true even for most unsurprised early opponents of the war, many of whom have been accused of wanting the Communists to win if for no other reason than to have their predictions come true. Typical of these is Susan Sontag, frequently denounced as being pro-Communist. After stating frankly that she was glad the war had ended as it did, she nevertheless found little taste for rejoicing, a feeling Mary McCarthy obviously shared, and expressed in one brief sentence: "The only beneficiaries I can see of the events of April 30 are the Vietnamese."

There is only one way for the American people also to become a beneficiary of these events: to accept what I consider to be the chief lessons of our involvement with Vietnam.

One obvious lesson is that, in matters of foreign policy, Americans must become more alert. Anything the government and the news media might say in defense of dubious aims must always be subjected to the most severe scrutiny. Vietnam has provided overwhelming evidence that, at this particular period in American history, there is one way to serve our nation's true interests: After listening not only to our government but also to its critics, an enlightened people must use the democratic process, including mass demonstrations, to fight what since the beginning of the "cold war" has become the essence of U. S. foreign policy.

To be more specific, I believe every thinking American should take seriously what a well-known authority on foreign policy, George Kennan, has to say in this context. Even for Americans who on occasion might favor the use of force to prevent an extension of Communist power, it should be easy to accept Kennan's warning "not to be hypnotized by the word 'Communism' and not to mess into other people's civil wars where there is no substantial American strategic interest at stake." It would indeed be a blessing for the United States if one result of Vietnam would be to prevent future administrations from "panicky and premature resort to force out of all proportion to the actual stakes involved" (Christopher Lasch). Although opposed to what could rightly be called Communist aggression, I too hope the United States will never again try to save reactionary dictatorships whose survival is threatened by popular uprisings.

It would be advisable for concerned Americans to take seriously the warning Prince Norodom Sihanouk issued more than three years before Nixon's decision to invade Cambodia: "The best way to make Communists is to put the American army into a place where there were no Communists before." This, of course, does not fully apply to Vietnam, where there were plenty of Communist long before the American army came and still made more. But it does apply to Cambodia, which today would probably not be Communist at all if Nixon had not ordered it invaded on April 30, 1970. As Sydney Schanberg put it in *The Saturday Review* of August 23, 1975: "The irony of American intervention in Cambodia is that it created the very kind of Communism it set out to contain."

Encouraging I found what pollster Lewis Harris wrote in the Paris *Herald Tribune* of September 12, 1975, about the result of a poll conducted by his organization: "Our people have come to believe that it is a mistake for us to back corrupt and repressive governments, no matter how beneficial the military advantages might be in such arrangements."

What I consider another important lesson of our failure in Vietnam is something I have practiced in my political life, as well as in my articles and books. Briefly stated, I have always been convinced, and am now more than ever, that in fighting Communism, sticking to political facts and historical truth is in the long run more effective than relying, as our leaders did in regard to Vietnam, on distortions and lies. In discussing America's Asian policy, the *London Sunday Times* wrote that "its massive lies ...have done as much to damage American Society and America's reputation as the failure of the policy itself."

It is to be hoped that America's political leaders will soon recognize what President Harry Truman, although not always practicing what he preached, regarded as the best way of fighting Communism. Elaborating on an earlier statement that national defense begins at home, this is what Truman (as quoted in an editorial of *The New York Times* of August 26, 1975) said in 1950: "We're vigorously pressing domestic programs to improve the standard of living of our people, to assure equal opportunity for all, to promote their health and education, and their security and freedom." Truman thought that we would have these programs "even if there were not a single Communist in the world," but he also regarded such programs as "the strongest anti-Communist weapons in our whole arsenal."

As regards those who preach to the American people what I call the wrong lessons of Vietnam, I shall deal only briefly with the fantastic distortion of historical truth by former governor of California, Ronald Reagan, speaking at a convention of the Veterans of Foreign Wars. After the U. S. had thrown three times as many bombs on Indochina as the Allies in World War II threw on their enemies, and after an American army of more than half a million soldiers, equipped with every existing kind of weapons, had been engaged in the longest and most brutal war Americans ever fought, Reagan wants the American people to believe that we failed in Vietnam because the Federal Government did not allow our fighting men to win the war. While Kissinger and Ford still try to put the blame for the "loss" of South Vietnam on Congress, Reagan, after the U. S. had also contributed to the decline of our economy by wasting at least 160 billion dollars, accuses the Federal Government of having "walked away" from the war.

I can think of only two possible explanations for this kind of statement by a man who wants to be president of the United States. Either he actually believes that Johnson, Nixon and Ford would not let our armed forces in Vietnam win the war, a belief which should finish him as their chief spokesman even in the eyes of his conservative followers; or he really knows better, revealing with his strange statement a truly outrageous degree of political irresponsibility.

More important and much more dangerous than Reagan's explanation of our failure in Vietnam, are the lessons drawn from it by Earl C. Ravenal in his article in *Foreign Affairs* of July, 1975. Although Ravenal claims that Americans are tired of lessons of Vietnam, the lessons he himself derives are more shocking than anything I have come across in my recent studies. One of these is implied in his complaint about "the constraints Congress and public opinion put on the actions of the executive." His fear that in similar instances in the future the executive will be subject to the same kind of constraint leads him to the conclusion that we must see to it that Congress and public opinion can never do this again. This of course would amount to giving up two essential conditions for the survival of any genuine democracy.

Still more important, because more frightening if accepted by a majority of America's political leaders, are two other lessons, or, as Ravenal calls them, "two divergent prescriptions" to be drawn from the American experience in Vietnam. In order to shore up the American position in the world, Ravenal thinks it might be necessary "to invite some demonstrative confrontation." And in order to restore credibility, he wants our government "to make stronger declaratory statements of our resolve."

Realizing the need to neutralize the adverse consequences he correctly expects from what he calls the restoration of America's "ability and propensity to use or threaten force" (which in this century only Hitler-Germany could boast of), Ravenal concludes, also correctly, that this would imply a conspicuously larger defense budget.

If many Americans were to accept Ravenal's views, Washington would soon start what Garry Wills is rightly afraid of, "a search for some place to prove our toughness." (An attempt toward that end was undoubtedly Ford's way of handling the Mayagues incident.) But to base America's foreign policy on what Ravenal calls his two prescriptions is conceivable only if the American people should ever accept life under a dictatorial and truly imperialistic regime.

I have long wondered how a man may be politically classified who wants the United States to pursue its foreign policy aims by using or threatening force, probably without realizing that, in the long run, this would prove incompatible with the survival of American democracy. Unable to come up with anything really adequate, I finally settled once again for the proposition that in politics a good mind, if dominated by ideologically-based preconceptions, can easily become a poor mind.

In conclusion, I quote John Kenneth Galbraith in his article in *The New York Times* of July 12, 1975: "You will ask why in relation to Hanoi the Chinese and Russians did better. One answer is that they were wiser: No Chinese or Russian troops were sent; no great body of advisors debouched . . . they were not thrown out because they were not there." To this I want to add that they were not there for reasons still not fully recognized by most Americans, one of these reasons being that they were not needed.

III.
Dominoes

This may be the place to discuss the "domino theory," so called ever since President Eisenhower, in April, 1954, said that "the loss of Indochina will cause the fall of Southeast Asia like a set of dominoes."

This theory has consistently been misinterpreted and is still being wrongly applied by most defenders of American intervention in Indochina. If taken seriously at all, there is only one way to correctly apply this theory: the countries of Southeast Asia which Eisenhower' expected to fall like dominoes were not those of Indochina. Since the countries he had in mind were to become dominoes only as a result of the "loss" of Indochina, by which Eisenhower meant Vietnam, Cambodia and Laos, the term domino could be properly applied only to the non-Indochinese countries of Southeast Asia—Thailand, Malaysia, Burma, Indonesia and the Philippines.

Not a single one of these Southeast Asian countries has fallen "like a domino" since the loss of Indochina, which was completed when the Communists, during the summer of 1975, were able effectively to establish their control also in Laos. And in the unlikely case that any of these countries should become Communist in the foreseeable future, this would not be the result of the "loss" of Indochina. What the domino theory completely ignored was the fact that Communist strength in Vietnam was a unique case in Southeast Asia. What happened in Vietnam after the end of World War II did not happen in any other Southeast Asian country, and is not likely to happen now. It will not happen, if it ever does, because of the "loss" of Indochina, but will rather be the result of conditions— economic, social and political—peculiar to each of these countries. Their instability, like that of many other countries of the so-called third world, is not primarily due to Communist subversion, but rather—again to quote Morgenthau—"from profound popular dissatisfaction with the social, economic and political status quo" (*The New Republic*, October 11, 1975).

However, some people, determined to disregard historical realities if they conflict with their political prejudices and wrong predictions, stubbornly cling to the domino theory, in spite of the fact that no "domino" has yet fallen. One of those people is George Meany who, after the fall of South Vietnam, stated: "The 'domino theory' is supposedly out of fashion, but events are reasserting it with a vengence." He could of course not claim that the "loss" of Indochina, as Eisenhower predicted, has caused any Southeast Asian "domino" to fall. His claim that recent events have reasserted the domino theory can therefore mean only that he considers— contrary to Eisenhower—South Vietnam, Cambodia and Laos as having been "dominoes." Apart from the fact that even for Meany South Vietnam could not have fallen as a domino if the United States had not made it one after 1954, Cambodia became Communist almost entirely, and Laos very largely, as a result not of Communist aggression but of American military intervention.

My view has for many years been that the effect of the fall of Indochina on other countries—and not only those of Southeast Asia—might possibly (as I hope) be the opposite of what the believers in the domino theory have been predicting. Since countries are likely to become falling dominoes not because of Communist subversion (though that may play a role) but because of the people's determination to get rid of corrupt, tyrannical and socially regressive regimes, our failure in Vietnam might convince some leaders in such countries that in order to avoid becoming falling dominoes they must base their regimes on popular support instead of on U. S. military presence. Only by becoming socially and politically progressive will they also become less vulnerable to the threat of Communism.' So far, unfortunately, there is little evidence that any of the leaders of those countries have learned this lesson.

Truly democratic and politically sophisticated Americans, opposed to Communism for better reasons than Vietnam's Thieu, Souharto of Indonesia, or Park of South Korea, have now a duty to their country and the whole world: they must intensify their struggle against an American foreign policy which, while claiming to defend freedom, continues to support tyrannical, inhuman, socially regressive, corrupt regimes.

IV.

Cambodia and Laos

These two countries, although dealt with in my previous books about the history of Indochina, have never been a concern of mine comparable to that of Vietnam. I have never been in Cambodia and Laos, and all my Indochinese political contacts and personal friends are Vietnamese. But since the struggle for Indochina ended with the victory of Communism not only in Vietnam but also in Cambodia and Laos, a few remarks about recent events in these two countries cannot be avoided.

Americans are still not fully aware that many Asians accept Communism for other reasons than those that lead a worker or intellectual in the Western world to join or sympathize with the Communist party, and that some social groups firmly opposed to Communism in the West cannot be mobilized in some Asian countries to fight against the establishment of a Communist regime.

This has to be kept in mind in any effort to explain why the Communists, under conditions quite different from those in Vietnam, were also successful in Cambodia and Laos.

I have already expressed my belief that there would today be no Communism in Cambodia if the United States had not interfered in that country, where the Communists were still a relatively weak political force before 1970. It was this intervention which, by creating a brutal and corrupt regime, and especially by recklessly bombing the country, prompted the people to join the Communist-led movement against the U. S.-created Lon Nol regime. Gradually becoming convinced that the war could end only through the victory of this movement, most Cambodians even welcomed North Vietnamese and Vietcong military assistance.

If reports from Phnom Penh, although not all verified, are even only partly true, the new Cambodian regime differed from the Provisional Revolutionary Government in Saigon in many respects, one of them being violence against some leaders of the defeated regime. But it differed from the new Saigon regime not only by using violence against its enemies—probably because it still lacked the organized strength and perhaps also the broad popular support the South Vietnamese Communists enjoyed. It also acted quite differently from the Saigon regime in getting the more than two million people who had fled to Phnom Penh out of the over-crowded capital and back into their villages. It is true that most of these people, if they had remained in Phnom Penh where they had suffered from a terrible lack of food even before the collapse of the Lon Nol regime, might have died of starvation. (On this subject, see the article by William Goodfellow in *The New York Times* of July 14, 1975.) It is also true that not only these refugees from the countryside, but even the soldiers "who marched into Phnom Penh, when asked what they wanted to do now, all said they just wanted to go home to their villages and farms again" (Sydney Schanberg, *Saturday Review*, August 23, 1975). Still, there is no excuse for the brutal manner in which the new rulers of Cambodia attacked this problem, quite contrary to the slow and careful way in which the same problem is being handled in Saigon. Even if some of the reports about the evacuation of Phnom Penh and the fate of the people driven into the countryside should turn out to have been exaggerated, this would still remain the saddest episode subsequent to the end of the war and the Communist victory in Indochina.

The fact that Asians may become Communists for other reasons than Westerners, and on the basis of different social and political conditions adopt different strategies for gaining power, becomes particularly evident in the way the Communists gradually made themselves masters of Laos, without resort to the kind of terror used by the Cambodian Communists, and no doubt because they met little resistance. While in Cambodia some officials of the defeated regime were killed, in Laos several non-Communist national leaders remained for awhile in a coalition dominated by the Communists. It seems that none of the Laotian right-wing and military leaders was executed, and that only those were condemned to death who had already become exiles in Thailand.

It is not possible to make any predictions about the future evolution of these two new and quite different Communist regimes, but what I am about to say as to how the United States should readjust its relations to Vietnam applies largely also to Cambodia and Laos.

V.
Correcting Past Errors and Repairing Past Wrongs

Is there a chance that, by recognizing the reasons for our failure in Indochina and by repairing some of the harm we have done, Washington can establish relations with Vietnam, Cambodia and Laos beneficial not only to these three countries but also to the United States? Establishing such relations and assisting in the reconstruction of Indochina would be a sure way to restore America's damaged reputation among people all over the world, including many in Communist countries.

This makes it necessary to bring up matters discussed in previous chapters—America's ignorance of Vietnamese history, ancient, colonial and contemporary. "The root cause of our Vietnam failure," Harvard professor John K. Fairbank believes, was "the profound American cultural ignorance of Vietnamese history, values, problems and motives when we originally went to the aid of the French in Vietnam after World War II." But Fairbanks does not think that we have learned much during the years of our sad experience in Indochina. "Now we are out, and still ignorant even of the depth of our ignorance."

Having for more than twenty years tried with books, brochures, articles and lectures to correct these misconceptions, I agree with those who think that Americans concerned about their country's future have a new, important duty: in order to understand why we failed in Vietnam, and to avoid a repetition of the same mistakes, we must now acquire a better knowledge not only of the history, the values and motivations of the Vietnamese people but also of other peoples whose future may affect our own, whether we regard them as enemies or allies.

Motivated by the same concern, Michael Harrington anticipated with surprising accuracy how the Vietnam war would end. In *Socialist America* he wrote in November 1972: "There is only one way in which those millions of agonies in Indochina can be given at least some retrospective meaning, if never a justification. That is if we resolve, in these days of mourning for a past that should not and need not have been, that it shall never happen again" (which sounds very much as if it has been written after April 1975).

The danger is great that Washington will continue on a road that can lead only to new disasters. Apparently with the same concern, *The New York Times* warned on May 7, 1975: "Past errors must not now be compounded by misreading of their meaning for the future."

There are well-meaning Americans who supported our Vietnam policy only out of ignorance or from a conviction that our leaders must have good reasons for pursuing this course. It is to be hoped that, shocked by the way it all ended, many of these Americans will now make the necessary effort to overcome their ignorance and also forswear the attitude of blind confidence in our leaders' knowledge and political wisdom. If studies toward that end are undertaken with an open mind, most Americans will come to the conclusion that it was stupid to get involved in Vietnam at all, and that what we did there was anti-democratic and inhuman. Only through such studies will we also find an answer to the perturbing question why, in this particular case, "America's enormous power proved to be impotent" (Stanley Karnow). Indeed, once the fundamental errors of our Vietnam policy are recognized, everything said and written about it since 1945 to justify first American support of the French and later our own military intervention becomes absolutely meaningless. And what a former influential governmental advisor, Walt Rostow, proposed only three weeks before the fall of Saigon—that we could still "save" South Vietnam if our marines invaded North Vietnam—will be generally recognized as foolish.

The fact that nobody, not even Ford and Kissinger, took Rostow's proposal seriously, seems to indicate that the American people had learned at least one important lesson from our failure in Vietnam: that the harm America may suffer from mistaken and usually also anti-democratic foreign policy decisions could only be made worse by sending our marines.

One reason why it should not be difficult for us to adopt an entirely new policy toward both North and South and an eventually reunited Communist Vietnam is that ideological preoccupations must not prevent the United States from exploiting the very real chances of counteracting Soviet and Chinese influence in Southeast Asia. An old Vietnamese acquaintance of mine, Phan Thien Chau, in America since 1958 and professor of political science at Rider College in New Jersey, wrote in the *Princeton Packet* after the fall of Saigon that Hanoi, in spite of the aid it received, is "not beholden to the Chinese and the Russians." Communist Vietnam, he predicts, will pursue an independent foreign policy.

This is also the opinion of Robert Shaplen, who underlines the fact that with its more than 40 million inhabitants and after capturing U. S. arms worth one billion dollars, Vietnam is now the most powerful nation in Southeast Asia (at least militarily). Not only Vietnam, but all of Indochina, Shaplen believes, "will almost surely adopt a 'Third World' posture", and will "balance itself adroitly between Russia and China."

Maynard Parker who, in his article in *Foreign Affairs* of January, 1975, accepts the likelihood of such a posture by the Vietnamese Communists, hints also at the effect this should have on America's foreign policy. After convincingly describing how reluctant Hanoi was, after the Paris cease-fire, to again seek victory on the battlefield, Parker speculates about the reasons for Hanoi's reticence. Convinced that Hanoi needs peace and help for the reconstruction of its cities and the revival of its economy, Parker says of these reasons, that "in them lies the best answer to America's future relationship with both Vietnams." He apparently also expected, already in January 1975, that after the end of the war Hanoi and Saigon would seek diplomatic relations with the United States, something which in the meantime has been confirmed by statements from Hanoi and Saigon.

This could not have come as a surprise to anyone familiar with contemporary Vietnamese history. I always expected that Hanoi, if only in order to keep a post-war Communist Vietnam reasonably independent of China and Russia, would again seek what Ho Chi Minh failed to achieve in 1945 and 1946: close diplomatic relations with the United States. For this reason alone I agree with Stanley Karnow, who in *The Saturday Review* of August 23, 1975, wrote:

"The United States could begin to set this process in motion by recognizing Hanoi and the Provisional Revolutionary Government in Saigon, and by initiating economic aid programs to both."

In the same issue of *The Saturday Review* Sydney Schanberg argues that this policy should also be extended to Cambodia. "On both humanitarian and pragmatic grounds, reconstruction aid would seem a policy worth considering. Not only would it help the Cambodian people at a time of great need, but it would also serve Washington's more practical interest in retaining influence in Asia."

Although I agree with *The New Republic's* editorial of May 3, 1975, that "no reparation we could pay will balance the evil we did there," reconstruction aid, especially for Vietnam, apart from creating sympathy for America among the Vietnamese people, would also do much to repair some of the damage America's reputation has suffered as a result of our Indochina policy. To help rebuild the countries we nearly destroyed should be recognized by the American people not only as a moral obligation, but no less as a policy more advantageous to U. S. interests in Southeast Asia than anything America has done in this part of the world since the end of World War II.

Is there a chance that Washington will move in that direction? Robert Shaplen thinks so. In his often quoted article in *The New Yorker* of May 19, 1975, Shaplen wrote: "Perhaps in a shorter time than it took us to come to terms with Communist China, we may make our adjustment to a new Vietnam and, whether out of guilt or for more sensible reasons, may establish a fresh relationship with the Communist Vietnamese and help in the rebuilding of the nation we devastated."

I am inclined to share this cautious optimism, but real progress in that direction cannot be expected as long as our responsible leaders fail to recognize that our Vietnam policy has been wrong from the very beginning. To recognize this should today be not too difficult for our leaders, even if they lack the political courage to admit their mistakes. But only by recognizing these mistakes will they be able to find better ways of securing a measure of American influence in Southeast Asia, better, that is, than the policy of supporting unpopular reactionary dictatorships.

It would of course strengthen the moral authority of America's political leadership, both at home and abroad, if those whose decisions caused so much harm not only to Indochina but also to their own country were willing to admit that they had been wrong. George Meany, much to his credit and to the surprise of many, has been one of the few who has made such a statement. At Dick Cavett's TV show, soon after the fall of Saigon, Meany said: "If I knew then what I know now, I would have been against the Vietnam war." But Meany, as John Herling pointed out in *The New Repblic* of October 4, 1975, has not gone far enough. After having, for at least a decade, "scorched union delegates who sought a clarification of the issues in Vietnam as being dupes of Communists," Meany still "has not publicly altered his opinion of those who were right when he was wrong."

This leads me, in conclusion, to state what has been a main objective in writing this book. I did not write it primarily to prove that those who opposed our Vietnam policy were right. My more ambitious aim, much harder to achieve, concerned those Americans who supported this policy, frequently only because they lacked the necessary information to resist governmental propaganda. Hoping that many of these normally well-meaning Americans will read this book, I tried my best to persuade them that they must re-examine their position and now determine for themselves why they had been wrong.

It should ease the political conscience of many former supporters of the war if they joined those who demand that the United States government honor its obligation to heal the wounds of war. In a letter to North Vietnam's Prime Minister Pham Van Dong, dated February 1, 1973, President Nixon promised American reconstruction aid, over a period of five years, to the amount of $3.25 billion—a sum which represents no more than 2 percent of what the United States spent for the war that destroyed so much of Vietnam.

It must serve as an inspiring example to all supporters of the war who have learned from the disastrous failure of their country's Vietnam policy that they were seriously mistaken, that many of them have joined those of their compatriots who have demanded unconditional amnesty for the young Americans who refused to fight in Vietnam.

Bibliography

In my first two historical works on Vietnam, covering more than two thousand years, I put together bibliographies of many hundred titles. Since this book covers events only from 1945 to the present, the number of books dealing with these events is of course much smaller.

Another important difference is that, of the the almost 600 titles listed in *The Smaller Dragon* (published in 1958), 490 are in French and less than 100 in English. This changed in the two-volume edition of *Vietnam: A Dragon Embattled* (published nine years later) to 188 titles in English and 124 in French, and even more drastically in my next two books. The bibliography of *Vietnam: A Political History* (published in 1968) contains 127 English and only 33 French titles, and in *A Dragon Defiant: A Short History of Vietnam* (published in 1972) only 13 out of 57 books are in French. But of the following bibliography consisting of 28 titles, only one is in French, and of the 27 titles in English only three are by other than American authors, underlining the fact that Vietnam has been for at least two decades a vital issue of American political history.

Almost all the books I list are by authors critical of or firmly opposed to the Vietnamese war. This is not primarily the result of my preference for such authors. It is surprising (and also encouraging) that of the books published on Vietnam during the past two decades by historians, political scientists and journalists, very few were written in defense of the Vietnamese war. I could find not more than two books to include in this bibliography whose authors try to justify American military intervention in Indochina.

American Friends Service Committee. *Peace in Vietnam: A New Approach in Southeast Asia.* Revised Edition, New York: Hill and Wang, 1967. A brief historical summary and proposal for a settlement.

Brown, Robert McAfee, Abraham Heschel, and Michael Novak. *Vietnam: Crisis of Conscience.* New York: Association Press, 1967. Statements of opposition to the war on religious and moral grounds.

Browne, Malcolm W. *The New Face of War.* Rev. ed. Indianapolis, Ind., and New York: The Bobbs-Merrill Company, 1968. About the failure of Diem's army to cope with the fighting techniques of the Vietcong and the decline of the Diem regime. The most important book on the nature of the war before the arrival of American combat troops.

Bruening, Ernest, and Herbert W. Beaser. *Vietnam Folly.* Washington, D.C.: The National Press, 1968. The Senator From Alaska, a longtime opponent of U.S. military intervention, forcefully argues his case.

Buttinger, Joseph, *Vietnam: A Political History.* New York: Praeger Publishers, 1968. A condensed edition of the author's three volume history, *The Smaller Dragon* and *Vietnam: A Dragon Embattled*, with a new chapter on the Americanization of the Vietnamese war.

Cooper, Chester L. *The Lost Crusade.* New York: Dodd, Mead and Company, 1970. A broad survey of U. S. involvement with Vietnam by a high Administration official-Assistant for Asian Affairs on the White House Staff and U. S. delegate at the Geneva Conference, 1954, and the 1961-62 Conference on Laos. Cooper tried hard to bring about a peaceful settlement of the Vietnamese war.

Devillers, Philippe. *Histoire du Viet-Nam de 1940 à 1952.* Paris: Editions du Seuil, 1952. The best account, by an author with first hand experience, of French policy in Vietnam during and after World War II. Indispensable for an understanding of the cause of Communist strength and the failure of the French in fighting the Vietminh.

Fall, Bernard B. *The Two Vietnams. A Political and Military Analysis.* 2nd. rev. ed. New York: Frederick A. Praeger, 1967. A critical account of both North and South Vietnam after 1954. Highly critical of the Diem regime and U. S. policy in Vietnam (The author was killed in Vietnam in February, 1967).

FitzGerald, Frances. *Fire in the Lake. The Vietnamese and The Americans in Vietnam.* An Atlantic Monthly Press Book. Little Brown and Company, Boston-Toronto, 1972. Probably the best survey of Vietnamese history and civilization, as well as a highly sophisticated description of the clash between American and Vietnamese culture, and one of the most convincingly critical interpretations of America's intervention in Vietnam.

Galbraith, John Kenneth. *How to Get Out of Vietnam: A Workable Solution to the Worst Problem of Our Time*. New York: New American Library, 1967. A "broadside," originally published in *The New York Times Magazine*.

Gavin, James M. (in collaboration with Arthur T. Hadley), *Crisis Now*. New York: Random House, 1968. A general's criticism of the "folly" of the Vietnam war and its ill effects on the United States.

Halberstam, David. *The Making of a Quagmire*. New York: Random House, 1965. South Vietnam as seen by the then *New York Times* correspondent. A devastating critic of the Diem regime, with a detailed description of the events prior to the overthrow of Diem by the army.

Hoopes, Townsend. *The Limits of Intervention*. New York: David McKay Company, 1970. An inside account of how the Johnson policy of escalation in Vietnam was reversed. Very important little-known information contained in Chapters 8 through 10.

In the Name of America. Published by the Clergy and Laymen Concerned About Vietnam. With contributions by Seymour Melman and Richard Falk. Annandale, Virginia: The Turnpike Press, Inc., 1968. A collection of documents showing how America's way of conducting the war in Vietnam violates all the rules of internationally agreed upon laws of war.

Kahim, George McTurnan, and John W. Lewis. *The United States in Vietnam*. New York: The Dial Press, 1967. An analysis of the history of America's involvement in Vietnam, aimed at destroying the assumptions underlying U.S. policy and propaganda.

Lacouture, Jean. *Vietnam: Between Two Truces*. Random House, 1966. With an introduction by Joseph Kraft. Chiefly a collection of articles, by one of the best informed Frenchmen, on both South and North Vietnam. Important information on the founding and composition of the National Liberation Front. Highly critical of the Diem regime.

Littauer, Raphael and Norman Uphoff (editors Air War Study Group Cornell University). *The Air War in Indochina* (Revised Edition). With a preface by Neil Sheehan. Beacon Press Boston, 1972. Everything known about the tonnage of bombs dropped, the cost of the bombing, the loss of planes and pilots, and the damage done to North Vietnam, South Vietnam, Laos and Cambodia.

Monroe, Malcolm. *The Means Is The End in Vietnam*. White Plains, N.Y.: Murlazan Press, 1968. A conservative lawyer, businessman and churchman condemning the Vietnamese war as "illegal and immoral."

The Pentagon Papers. The complete and unabridged series as published by *The New York Times*. Based on investigative reporting by Neil

Sheehan. Written by Neil Sheehan, Hedrick Smith, E. W. Kenworthy, and Fox Butterfield. With Key Documents and 64 pages of photographs. New York: Bantam Books, Inc., 1971.

Pettit, Clyde Edwin. *The Experts.* Secaucus, N.J.: Lyle Stuart, Inc., 1975. A collection of statements, made mostly by French and American so-called experts (military and political between 1940 and 1973). The author's purpose is to show that all optimistic statements about the first and second Indochina wars have been proved wrong by events.

Raskin, Marcus G., and Bernard B. Fall (eds). *The Vietnam Reader.* Rev. ed. New York: Random House, 1968. Articles and documents on Vietnam and U.S. foreign policy.

Salisbury, Harrison E. *Behind the Lines—Hanoi.* New York: Evanston, and London: Harper and Row, 1967. The first report by an American on the effect, material, moral and political, of the bombing of North Vietnam.

Schell, Jonathan. *The Military Half: An Account of Destruction in Quang Ngai and Quang Tin.* New York: Alfred A. Knopf, 1968. What American planes and artillery are doing to the country and people of South Vietnam.

Schlesinger, Arthur M., Jr. *The Bitter Heritage: Vietnam and American Democracy, 1941–1966.* Boston: Houghton Mifflin Company, 1966. A balanced criticism of America's Vietnam policy and a plea for a negotiated settlement of the war.

Shaplen, Robert. *The Lost Revolution: The U.S. in Vietnam, 1946–1966.* Rev. ed. New York: Harper and Row, 1966. The comments of one of America's best-informed observers and students of contemporary Vietnamese history. Especially important is the chapter on the 1963 crisis that led to the end of the Diem regime.

Stavins, Ralph, Richard J. Barnet, and Marcus G. Raskins. *Washington Plans An Aggressive War.* A documented account of the United States adventure in Indochina. New York: Vintage Books (a Division of Random House), 1971. Highly critical of what the authors call "this horrendous chapter in our history." Part I: *Washington Determines the Fate of Vietnam* by Ralph Stavins contains probably the most important information about the way U.S. military intervention was decided upon and prepared between 1954 and 1965. (The book is dedicated to the memory of Bernard Fall, whom the authors describe as "scholar and friend, who gave his life to find out the truth about the Indochina war.")

Taylor, Maxwell D. *Responsibility and Response.* New York: Harper and Row, 1967. A brief account of U.S. policy in Southeast Asia by the General and former Ambassador to South Vietnam. A defense of American policy in Vietnam.

Trager, Frank N. *Why Vietnam?* New York: Frederick A. Praeger, 1966. A routine defense of U.S. policy with a brief historical introduction.

Of the books on recent events in Vietnam which have appeared since I finished *Vietnam: The Unforgettable Tragedy,* I want to add the following two to this bibliography:

Porter, Gareth. *A Peace Denied.* Bloomington and London: Indiana University Press, 1975. Porter produces conclusive evidence for the view that U. S. support of President Thieu's sabotage of the Paris Agreement of January 1973 prolonged the war and prevented the negotiated political solution of the conflict provided for in the agreement.
Terzani, Tiziano. *Giai Phong! The Fall and Liberation of Saigon.* New York: St. Martin's Press, 1976. Readers will find this the most informative book on the events immediately prior to and during the first three months after the fall of Saigon on April 30, 1975. These events are also illustrated by 57 photographs.

Index

PRODUCTION NOTE

This book has been set in Janson by Cemar Graphic Designs Ltd.
of Rockville Centre, New York,
Printing and binding were done by Noble Offset Printers
of New York, New York.
Book designed by Sidney Solomon